D0734376

OTHER BOOKS BY WILFERD A. PETERSON

The Art of Living
The New Book of the Art of Living
More About the Art of Living
Adventures in the Art of Living

A SEARCH FOR
A WAY OF LIFE
FOR THESE TIMES

The Art of
Living
in the World
Today

by Wilferd A. Peterson

SIMON AND SCHUSTER
NEW YORK

*Copyright © 1969 by Wilferd A. Peterson
Published by Simon and Schuster
Rockefeller Center, 630 Fifth Avenue
New York, New York 10020*

The author wishes to express appreciation and thanks to the
following for their permission to quote from the
sources mentioned:
Bess Streeter Aldrich, *A Lantern in Her Hand,*
copyright © 1956 by Appleton-Century-Crofts.
Thomas Dreier, *The Religion of a Vagabond,*
copyright 1947 by Harper & Row, Publishers.
Edwin Markham, "Outwitted," from *Poems of Edwin Markham*
selected and arranged by Charles L. Wallis. Published
by Harper and Company, 1950, and reprinted by
permission of Virgil Markham.
Ashley Montagu, *Man in Process,* copyright © 1961. Published
by World Publishing Co.

FIRST PRINTING

SBN 671–20339–8
*Library of Congress Catalog Card Number: 72–84129
Designed by Irving Perkins
Manufactured in the United States of America
Printed by United Lithographing Co., New York, N. Y.
Bound by H. Wolff, New York, N. Y.*

ACKNOWLEDGMENTS

My sincere thanks to my wife, Ruth, whose inspiration, encouragement and suggestions contributed immeasurably to the writing of this book; to my editor, Henry W. Simon, for his patience, understanding and guidance; and to Inspiration, Good Business *and* Science of Mind *magazines for permission to use and adapt several of my writings that originally appeared in these publications.*

Dedicated to the memory of
REV. LAWRENCE G. NEWHOUSE,
who radiated the love and
goodness of God

TABLE OF CONTENTS

To finish the moment, to find the journey's end
in every step of the road, to live
the greatest number of good hours is wisdom.
Since our office is with moments, let
us husband them. Five minutes of today
are worth as much to me as five minutes
in the next millennium. Let us
be poised and wise and our own, today.

—RALPH WALDO EMERSON

A PERSONAL NOTE
FROM THE AUTHOR

Y OU will notice that the essays in this book are different from those in the other Art of Living books I have written. Let me tell you about it.

The first four Art of Living books were written in a prose-poetry style—brief sentences, short paragraphs, each essay consisting of only three hundred words or so. The little books, beautifully designed and printed, are aimed to give *"instant inspiration."* They are created for odd-moment reading, and the fact that over 800,000 copies are in print today indicates that they fill a need.

But many letters asked that I go further. Readers suggested that I write a book of longer essays giving more sustained thought to a philosophy of the art of living. People asked me about the dynamics of creative thought, about my personal religious philosophy; they asked how spiritual power can be applied to living in these days of pressure and tension, how we can meet the crises of our times, how we can inspire a new idealism in our youth, find a faith to live by. . . .

So this is how this distinctly different Art of Living book came to be written. In a way, I suppose you might say that this book is my spiritual autobiography. The printed words express how I think about many things. I pass them on here, not because I expect you to agree with me, but simply to set down one man's thoughts about the adventure of life.

Because this book touches just about all the facets of life we have entitled it *The Art of Living in the World Today*. If in these pages you discover some guidelines to living more triumphantly, this will be my greatest reward.

WILFERD A. PETERSON
1721 Woodward Avenue, S.E.
Grand Rapids, Michigan

THE ART OF LIVING IN THE WORLD TODAY

THE world we have been born into is the only world we have. Our world today is the most unpredictable, turbulent, changeable and dangerous world in which man has ever lived. It is also the most adventurous. We cannot stop the world and get off. We cannot escape its problems and pressures. Our challenge is to face up heroically to the world as it is and do our very best to make the most of our lives. To strive to live each day with serenity and courage. To develop a creative faith for these times. To hang on to the unshakeable things in life. To preserve a personal world of sanity and maturity amidst the outer world of confusion. To contribute the humble ounces of our weight to help tip the scale toward all that we deem good in our common life. The purpose of this book is to explore with you the art of living in the world today.

One of the great dangers of the nuclear stalemate of terror under which we live today is that we will sacrifice our future to fear.

There are many young people who feel that a nuclear holocaust is inevitable, that there is little chance for them to live out their lives. Facing what to them seems to be a hopeless situation, they show a tendency to surrender their ideals and to retreat from their aims and objectives.

Whenever I have an opportunity to speak to high school and college students I ask them: "What if five years from now you awake as from a bad dream to find that the expected holocaust hasn't happened? You may have given up college and the beginning of a successful career. You find that you have wasted your life in futile fear. For many of you the hour may be late to make up lost ground. You will live in a hell of regret and remorse."

I then plead with these young people to continue to live day after day as though the possibility of nuclear war did not exist. I remind them that Alfred North Whitehead said: "It is the duty of the future to be dangerous," and that progress seems to demand it. "You cannot hide from nuclear missiles," I tell them, "but you can ignore them and go courageously about the business of living your life. You can erase them from your mind. Continue to follow your dream."

"This way," I go on, "you have everything to gain and nothing to lose. If we avoid nuclear war, and pray God we shall, you will be on your way. You will have made the most of every moment that is yours, to grow and serve and enjoy life. You will have completed your education, started a home, found happiness. If somewhere along the way the worst should happen, you will have the satisfaction of knowing that you fulfilled yourself in the time allotted to you and that you transcended your fears."

On one of my birthdays my ten-year-old granddaughter sent me a birthday card in which she had written a personal note. "Dear Gramps," it said, "I hope you live all your life." That's about it. There are no guarantees, no infallible guards against danger and disease, no positive security. Our objective should be to live, really live, all the days of our lives, through joys, disasters, threats, sunshine and storm. To make the most of our lives—this is the very heart of the art of living.

One day while reading an essay by Henry David Thoreau, I chanced on a sentence he had written when he beheld the woodsman's ax destroying the forests he loved. "Thank God," he wrote, "they cannot cut down the clouds!"

There are other eternal things besides clouds that the destructive powers of man, in all their fury, cannot destroy. To think on these things is to achieve an inner quiet and peace in the midst of confusion. There is no confusion among the stars. The sun still rises and sets. The mountains are not disturbed. Birds sing. Little streams dance merrily on their way to the sea. Flowers bloom and give of their perfume. The world goes right on being a beautiful place.

There are indestructible qualities of the human spirit, too. Mother love is immortal and though crushed to earth will rise again. Courage shines through the blackest night. Faith gallantly rides the whirlwinds sweeping the earth.

You cannot cut down the clouds. The spirit of man cannot be destroyed. The finest things of life are immortal . . . they will survive. To recognize this truth in the complex, burden-troubled world in which we live today gives a lift and lilt to life.

Sigmund Freud once wrote a letter to Princess Marie Bonaparte in which he said: "The moment a man questions the meaning and value of life he is sick." In all our ups and downs it is essential that we continue to believe in life and its possibilities, in its improvableness, in the miracles that can come to pass. Life opens up for those who hold an attitude of creative expectancy of good.

Emerson was a wise observer when he wrote: "We are

always getting ready to live, but never living." A psychologist, William Moulton Marston, made a survey of 3,000 people that proves this point. Ninety-four percent of those surveyed were merely enduring the present while they waited for the future, waited for conditions to change, waited for children to grow up, waited for debts to be paid, waited for retirement to come. They postponed living while life passed them by. I once read a beautiful sentence by Marie Beynon Ray that we should all memorize and remind ourselves of each day: "We have only the present moment, sparkling like a star in our hands—and melting like a snowflake."

I think one of the finest examples of a man who made the most of each moment and lived all his life was St. Francis of Assisi. He was a genius of the mind and spirit. He was the founder of the Franciscan order of monks who went about doing good. So joyous were they that they were known as "God's troubadours." St. Francis felt a kinship not only with men but with every bird and star and flower. They were his brothers and sisters. He believed that the cause of peace began with a positive love of peace in the human heart. His constant prayer was: "Lord, make me an instrument of Thy peace. . . ."

Once someone came to this master of the art of living while he was working in his garden, and asked: "Brother Francis, what would you do if you were suddenly told that the world would come to an end at sunset today?" St. Francis didn't hesitate for a moment. His answer was clear and simple: "I would go on hoeing my garden."

To live life fully, completely, bravely, straight through to the end . . . this is to make an art of life.

Let us now consider what I believe to be the three vital areas into which the art of living is divided.

The Art of Living with Ourselves

Wrote the poet and mystic Maeterlinck: "The thoughts you think will irradiate you as though you are a transparent vase." We radiate what we *are* and so it is more important to *be* than to *get*, to *become* than to *possess*. People tune in to our inner wave length. There is much wisdom in the old Hindu saying: "Beware, beware, beware, what goes forth from you will come back to you."

As a boy I learned a little rhyme that I have never forgotten: "Don't be veneer stuck on with glue, be solid mahogany all the way through."

Our first task then, in living with ourselves, is to be ourselves, to be genuine and sincere, to go forth to others as the persons we truly are without sham or pretense. Beyond this our task is to grow in mind and spirit.

While driving on the Ohio Turnpike I saw a sign exhorting drivers. "Stay Awake, Stay Alive," it cried. These words, it seems to me, have even deeper significance as a way of life. The more awake we are to what goes on around us the more alive we will be. Being wide awake opens the way to experiencing the infinite riches of body, mind, heart and spirit.

We do not sufficiently use the senses God has given us. The magazine *ETC*, the quarterly review of the International Society of General Semantics, devoted a full issue to the subject of LSD and other psychedelic drugs. Editor S. I. Hayakawa made this vital point: "Most people haven't learned to use the senses they possess. I not only hear music, I *listen* to it. I find the colors of the day such vivid experiences that I sometimes pound the steering wheel with excitement. And I say why disorient your beautiful senses with drugs and poisons before you have half discovered what they can do for you?"

The great mystics did not fog up the windows of heaven with drugs. They did not distort their visions with poisons. They found their own senses and their perceptive and intuitive powers sufficient to experience the Presence of God.

To make the most of ourselves we must become aware of the miracles all around us. We must open our eyes, ears, minds, hearts, spirits. We must think about great ideas such as space illimitable, time everlasting, energy inexhaustible. You have the magic power within yourself to broaden your horizons, to lift your consciousness, to live more abundantly.

To learn to live with ourselves we must often get away by ourselves so we can find quiet, solitude and time to think and meditate.

The poet Robert Frost stressed the importance of separateness. He told a group, of which I was a part, that we must be careful that we do not homogenize society as we homogenize milk . . . so the cream at the top disappears. The heart and the lungs work together, he explained, but they are also separate organs. A man, he said, should endeavor to achieve separateness in his thinking, even amidst the pressures of the crowd. And often we may experience a greater feeling of togetherness with people when we are separate and alone, rather than with others. We must learn to live together, but we must not lose the precious gift of separateness.

The growth of the self, however, is not accomplished only in solitude and isolation. Aloneness must be balanced with contacts with people and the world. There is need to try out our ideas on others, to sharpen our minds, to contend with those who disagree with us. We can learn from our enemies as well as our friends, and often those who are hardest on us contribute more to our growth than those who make things easy for us.

I have always liked these words attributed to Walt Whitman: "Have you learned lessons only of those who admired you and were tender with you and stood aside for you? Have you not learned great lessons from those who braced themselves against you, and disputed the passage with you?"

The self needs the spur of conflict, competition, even defeat, for out of these come strength and character.

Heed these words by Epictetus: "So when the crisis is upon you, remember that God, like a trainer of wrestlers, has matched you with a tough and stalwart antagonist—that you may be a winner at the Great Games."

The art of living with ourselves also requires that we be resilient and flexible so we will not break ourselves against the hardness of life. I learned this important lesson from a naturalist in Bryce Canyon, Utah. I asked him about the gallant lone pines on the mountaintops that survive the full sweep of wind and storm.

I was told that the pines are called Limber Pines. To demonstrate, the naturalist took a branch of a Limber Pine and tied it into a knot. In a few minutes he untied the knot and the branch immediately sprang back to its original position.

It is not through never bending that the trees survive. It is in never failing to spring erect again after the gale has passed that victory is achieved.

Resiliency is also an important factor in the art of living with ourselves. The winds of life—the conflicts, pressures, changes—will bend us, but if we have resiliency of the spirit they cannot break us. To courageously straighten up again after our heads have been bowed by defeat, disappointment and suffering is a supreme test of character.

To learn to live with ourselves, to make the most of ourselves, to achieve wholeness of personality, to grow into more effective human beings—this is the first vital step in the art of living.

The Art of Living with Others

The secret of living successfully with others is not in the practice of certain surface techniques and assumed attitudes. Harmony within ourselves comes first in learning to live harmoniously with others.

Beyond this, in my personal relationships with people and the world, I have found help and guidance from an anthropologist and a philosopher. They opened my eyes to two great truths about living together—the reality of brotherhood and the oneness of life.

The brotherhood of man is usually thought of as something unattainable, the vision of a dreamer. The truth is that brotherhood exists now and has always existed. The brotherhood of man is here. It is not a fancy but a fact. It is not a dream but a reality.

Ashley Montagu, the anthropologist, tells us that there is no such thing as race, that all men spring from common ancestors. "The existing varieties of mankind," he writes, "are derived from the same ancestral group and belong to a single species. So far as the mental traits of the variety of mankind are concerned, it is now quite certain such traits are not linked with physical characteristics, and it is reasonably certain that those behavioral traits which are alleged to be racial or inborn are acquired by social heredity and not by biological inheritance. The genetic structure of mankind is so alike that the conclusion would, on this ground alone, seem inescapable—that all men are brothers under the skin."

What about differences in the chemistry of the blood? Montagu answers: "Fundamentally the blood of all human beings is similar, no matter what class, group, nation or 'race' they belong to. Obviously then, since all people are of one blood, such differences as may exist between them have absolutely no connection with blood."

Children do not begin to hate until we teach them to

hate, until we create environments that instill hatred in their minds and hearts. There is absolutely no such thing as a *born* bigot. Hatred, resentment, prejudice, intolerance—all are acquired attitudes.

In living with others on this earth we need at last to recognize the *reality* of brotherhood. We *are* brothers. We share a common fate. In this nuclear age we will live or die together. To become aware of this fact should inspire us to do our best to break down the mental walls of prejudice, fear and misunderstanding that separate us, so that we may live together and work together to achieve our mutual objectives and realize our full potentials as human beings.

Man is not naturally warlike. The thought patterns, habits, emotions, ideals that motivate him are acquired. Because man is a brother to his fellow man it is high time he began *thinking* and *acting* like a brother. Not all men will recognize the fact of brotherhood, but those who do should not wait for others to do something but should begin at once to put the spirit of brotherhood into action. There will be many disappointments, defeats and discouragements, but we must continue to try to bring men together. Only if we do this can we hope to survive in this dangerous world. *We must stop incorrect thinking before incorrect thinking stops us.*

Albert Schweitzer agrees with Montagu about the oneness of life and gives us a philosophical approach to that oneness. Schweitzer, who died at ninety, was a medical missionary in Africa. He was also an organist, an authority on Bach, a theologian and a philosopher. His greatest teaching is compressed into a spiritual capsule of three words.

While at his hospital in Africa he worked evenings on his books on the philosophy of civilization. He continued searching for a condensed statement that would embody a universal ethic for man. The words he sought came to him while he was journeying up the Ogowe River in Africa. He had been writing ideas on a pad. Suddenly his mind lighted up with the phrase: *reverence for life.*

When one has reverence for life, he holds life in the highest esteem as God's gift to man. He recognizes that all life is a part of God and that God is a part of all life. He sees that the chief purpose of life—plant, animal and human—is to express itself. The universal affirmation of all life is the will to live, to grow, to make the most of its own unique qualities.

When a man has reverence for life, he will never do anything to harm, hinder or destroy life. Instead he bends every effort to help life to fulfill its highest destiny. He strives to maintain, enhance and assist life to make the most of itself.

When we take the phrase *reverence for life* into our minds and think about it, our consciousness is lifted up. We see that when we help other men we help ourselves, because we are one, we are a part of each other. We come to realize that when we war on life we war on ourselves, for the same life flows through all men.

Reverence for life means helping men, healing men, teaching men, inspiring men, leading men. . . . It is having the vision to see that when even the very smallest segment of life is helped, all life is helped. It is using our influence to glorify and celebrate the eternal miracle of life.

The keys of brotherhood and reverence for life will unlock the door to new horizons in the creative relationship of men.

The Art of Living with God

This is the third vital area in the art of living. No man lives to himself alone, and I believe that the power of God's goodness can become a dynamic force in the living of each day.

A story I heard about Woodrow Wilson started a train of thought in my mind which was further expanded by a visit to Grand Coulee Dam. . . . Woodrow Wilson lay dying, his dream of America's leadership in establishing peace in the world toppled and crushed. His country had refused to become a part of the League of Nations which he had conceived. When interviewed and asked his thoughts as he surveyed the destruction of his hopes, Wilson raised himself on an elbow, shook a bony finger and said, *"They cannot stop God!"*

And yet isn't this what man has been doing through all the ages—*stopping God? The littleness of men gets in the way of the bigness of God.* We have set up barriers of fear, prejudice, suspicion, hatred, which have prevented the goodness of God from breaking through. We have expected God to work miracles directly from heaven, when He can only work them *through men.* When Martin Buber was asked, "Where is God?" he replied, "God is wherever men will let Him in."

What is man's role in becoming a channel for God's goodness? This was the question I asked myself. And then came a revealing experience which I wish to share with you. . . .

One day my wife and I drove over the beautiful Columbia River Highway. At times we were high above the river as it flowed between the mountains. At other times we were down near the shore. The water was turbulent as it flowed through the rapids; again it moved quietly but relentlessly on its way to the sea. Here was a river of tremendous potential power ready and waiting to be used by men. And then we came to Grand Coulee Dam. A guide took us in an elevator far down below the dam. Here he showed us seven giant converters. These converters, we were told, convert the waters of the Columbia River into electrical power to light the great Northwest, to turn the wheels of industry, to supply energy for the operation of millions of household appliances. The converters put the potential power of the Columbia River to work.

There is another river. It is the Golden River of God's love, wisdom and goodness. It, too, has unlimited potential power. It is inexhaustible. It will never cease to flow. It is an eternal source of power instantly available to man. But, just as the Columbia River must be converted into electrical energy, the Golden River of God must be converted into spiritual energy.

Man's role, then, is to serve as a human converter of the Golden River of God's goodness. God is invisible until man converts God's goodness into *visible* acts. Man converts God's goodness by using it, by applying it to life, by expressing it. Man first removes the barriers of limited and negative thinking, freeing the channel for the inflow of the unlimited supply of goodness in the universe. Then he converts that goodness, putting it to work in creative thought and action. He converts God's infinite goodness into spiritual electricity to light up the world.

In Boris Pasternak's masterpiece on the Russian Revolution, the novel *Dr. Zhivago,* he has the doctor remark: "I used to be very revolutionary, but now I know that nothing can be gained by brute force. People must be drawn to goodness by goodness."

The supreme function of man in living in partnership with God is to convert God's goodness into tangible acts, to create a better life for man.

In this first essay we have endeavored to explore the three vital areas in the art of living . . .

First, to *be* more. To grow personally toward your ideal.

Second, to have reverence for all life and help it to express itself.

Third, to light up the world by converting God's goodness into spiritual electricity.

And so at the end of this essay we are really at the beginning. For now we must go out and *live* it.

DEEP OPTIMISM

RECENTLY I heard a speech that shook me up and started the processes that led to the thoughts I am passing on here.

The speaker said, "The trouble with Americans is that we think everything will come out all right. We haven't the courage to face facts. We haven't the sense of tragedy that Europe has. We are puffed up with self-importance. We think we are somebody and we like to strut. Yet a tiny bacillus that can be seen only through the most powerful microscope can kill a man. And our earth is so small that locating it in the solar system would be like flying a plane down the Mississippi Valley looking for a particular grain of sand. Let's quit kidding ourselves about being powerful. We are weak. Let's face the world with humility."

This opened up to me the whole area of optimism versus pessimism. As I think about it, it seems to me there are two kinds of optimism. First, there is shallow optimism. This is the back-slapping, keep-your-chin-up, Pollyanna type of optimism. Basically, it is the refusal to face reality. Such so-called optimists are usually found wanting when the test comes. This kind of optimism is primarily a surface quality and often when we scratch the surface we find a pessimist. It is based on the silly assumption that "the man worthwhile is a man who can smile when everything goes dead wrong."

Shallow optimism has been defined in these words: "An optimist is one who doesn't care what happens as long as it doesn't happen to him." When it happens to him, that is different. He is always hiding his head in the sand. He closes his eyes to reality. As the poet Douglas Malloch has said, "An optimist is one who sees a light where there isn't any and a pessimist is a man who comes along and blows out the light."

There is another kind of optimism that has built civilization. It could well be called *deep optimism*. Deep optimism has strong roots in the goodness of God. It is anchored in love, hope, courage and faith. The deep optimist responds heroically to every test. He realizes that he cannot control everything that happens to him but that he can control his response to what happens to him.

It has been said that the pessimist is often more finely made than the optimist. That he is more sensitive and aware of life's trials, tribulations, fears and problems. He sees the tremendously complex and involved situations of our civilization. He sees the tasks to be done, and often they seem overwhelming. He may express discouragement and despair, but in his reaction he is a deep optimist. Deep down he never surrenders. He never lowers his sights. He never changes the direction of his life. No matter what the odds may be against victory, he throws the full influence of his life on the side of the good.

He may talk pessimism but he *lives* optimism.

The important thing is not to see the future through rose-colored glasses when the future isn't truly rose colored. To cope with life, we must face up to it in all of its stark reality. We must make our lives count for the highest and best no matter how dark the future may appear to be.

Abraham Lincoln was a sensitive, melancholy man. His biographers say he never carried a penknife for fear he might take his own life.

Yet what a deep optimist Lincoln was! Failure couldn't defeat him.

As a young man he ran for the legislature in Illinois and was badly swamped. He next went into business with a man who ran a store in the little village of New Salem, Illinois. The business failed, and Lincoln spent many years paying off the debts of a worthless partner. He was in love with a beautiful woman, Ann Rutledge, to whom he became engaged. Then she died.

Entering politics again, he ran for Congress and was again defeated, although later he ran for Congress and was elected and served one term. He tried to get an appointment to the United States Land Office and again he failed. In 1856 he became a candidate for Vice President and again went down in defeat. In 1858 he ran for the Senate against Douglas and was defeated.

Failure after failure, but Lincoln did not give up, and he went on to become a great president and to be called "A Man for the Ages."

During the dark days of the Civil War, Lincoln said, "The dogmas of the quiet past are inadequate to the stormy present. The occasion is piled high with difficulty and we must rise with the occasion. Our case is new, so we must think anew and act anew." How vibrant and challenging these words are for us in this nuclear age!

The deep optimist rises to the occasion, meets the challenge of his times.

Think of George Washington and his troops buried in the snows of Valley Forge during the American Revolution. The soldiers were ragged and barefoot; suffering was intense. Many deserted and returned to their homes. Things never looked so dark for the new nation. What a time for deep optimism!

Thomas Paine, sitting by a campfire, using a drumhead as a desk, wrote an inspiring message for those dark days—"These are the times that try men's souls. The summer soldier and the sunshine patriot will, in this crisis, shrink from the service of his country; but he that stands it *now,* deserves the love and thanks of man and woman. Tyranny, like hell, is not easily conquered; yet we have this consolation with us, that the harder the conflict, the more glorious the triumph."

We owe our freedom to deep optimists of the caliber of George Washington and Thomas Paine.

During the Second World War, after Dunkirk and the fall of France, England stood alone against Hitler. German planes with their incendiary bombs were over England every night. A time for despair? A time to give up? Listen to the eloquent words of Winston Churchill, spoken at Bristol University, April 12, 1941: "I go about the country whenever I can escape for a few hours or a day from my duty at headquarters, and I see the damage done by the enemy attacks; but I also see side by side with the devastation and amid the ruins the quiet, confident, bright and smiling eyes, beaming with the consciousness of being associated with a cause far higher and wider than any human or personal issue. I see the spirit of an unconquerable people. I see a spirit bred in freedom, nursed in a tradition that has come down to us through the centuries, and which surely at this moment, this turning point in the history of the world, will enable us to bear our part in such a way that none of the race who come after us will have any reason to cast reproach upon their sires." Deep optimism again, saving the world.

When we read the history of science and discovery, we learn that success often came as the result of hundreds, and often thousands, of experiments. As they failed, time after time, the scientists no doubt often expressed disappointment and discouragement. They might have been pessimistic about the outcome, but they never stopped experimenting. They were deep optimists.

Consider Thomas Edison, who tested materials from all over the world in his search for a filament for his incandescent lamp until he finally made a cotton carbonized thread glow for over forty hours in a glass tube. Today we can press a button and flood a room with light because Edison was a deep optimist.

It took Christopher Columbus five years to raise money for ships to sail on his voyage of discovery. He finally persuaded Queen Isabella of Spain to sell her jewels to help him. As he sailed onward through the treacherous and unknown seas, his men planned mutiny. Columbus, with his courage and faith, inspired them to sail onward. Here was a dramatic demonstration of deep optimism.

Back in the seventeenth century Galileo developed the first telescope. He put two lenses in a copper tube. His first telescope magnified to twice normal size. Later he developed a telescope that stepped up magnification thirty-two times. He pointed the telescope into the night sky and discovered that the Milky Way was not a streak of light but a multitude of stars. Tried by the Inquisition for his beliefs, Galileo was declared a heretic and forced to recant.

Other deep optimists since Galileo's pioneering effort have achieved unbelievable progress in astronomy. The Hale Telescope on Mount Palomar in California gathers within the circle of its 200-inch mirror a million times as much starlight as the unaided eye can see. It will reflect light from stars billions of light years from earth, recording this reflection on film for scientists to study. And today, through the vision and faith of deep optimists, we are actually venturing forth to explore outer space.

On December 17, 1903, the Wright brothers made the first powered plane flights at Kitty Hawk, North Carolina. Orville Wright made the first attempt, and his plane was in the air only twelve seconds, covering a distance of 120 feet. Later the same day Wilbur Wright kept his plane in the air for fifty-nine seconds and flew 852 feet. These two men, makers of bicycles, had a deep faith that man could fly, and they made their dream come true. Last Christmas, I flew from Los Angeles to Hawaii in a little over five hours in a modern jet traveling almost 600 miles an hour. Think of the multitude of obstacles overcome by deep optimists to make possible our progress in aviation, and now man is traveling through space to the moon!

Today our nation is on wheels. Back in 1888, Henry Ford built his first car from old bicycle wheels, gas pipe and a cylinder from an old steam engine. He put the car together in the shed behind his home, and when he went for his trial ride he found that he had forgotten to put a reverse gear in the car. For years, this was the only car on the streets of Detroit. Ford called his wife "The Believer" because she believed in him and in his future. Here, in these lowly beginnings, the great automobile industry was born. Another contribution by a deep optimist.

In the area of art, Michelangelo stands supreme. In sculpture, his giant statues of David and of Moses are outstanding masterpieces. He created the painting on the ceiling of the Sistine Chapel in Rome, considered the greatest achievement in the whole history of art. For four years, Michelangelo worked on this project, lying on his back on a scaffold. Sometimes he worked at night, with candles fastened to a cardboard hat. Often he slept on the scaffold and had his food drawn up by a rope. He

29

painted the Creation and the Fall of Man in 343 figures, larger than life. Only deep optimism, deep faith and complete dedication could achieve such miracles.

Consider Robert Louis Stevenson and his contribution to literature. Dying of tuberculosis, hemorrhaging frequently, yet holding death at bay, he wrote such immortal masterpieces as *Treasure Island* and *Dr. Jekyll and Mr. Hyde*. Writers must of necessity be deep optimists, for there are few writers who have achieved success before they have collected sufficient rejection slips to paper the room in which they write. Consider Thomas Carlyle, who wrote his great book *The French Revolution,* representing years of research and toil, only to have a servant accidentally throw the entire manuscript into the fire. And consider the deep optimism of a man with the courage to rewrite the entire book.

The history of medicine represents an age-old struggle of deep optimists working in the battle against disease. Consider Pasteur, crippled from a stroke, battling to win recognition for his germ theory. Did you ever visit an old cemetery with graves dating back into the last century and see where whole families were wiped out by diphtheria and small pox, diseases which today have been conquered? Consider the long, discouraging battle against polio which was finally won through the development of the new vaccines. Consider the long struggle toward enlightenment in the treating of the mentally ill, from the "insane asylums" of the past to the mental hospitals of today. Consider, too, the miracles that are being achieved today in heart surgery and transplants. Consider the widening scope and the continuing effort to develop new drugs, new techniques, new therapies in the battles against all diseases of the body and the mind.

The record of every forward movement is a record of conquest over difficulties.

The shallow optimists give up. The deep optimists never stop trying even when causes seem to be lost.

Deep optimism runs like a golden thread through the whole story of the progress of man on this earth.

Recently I sat in a darkened church looking up at a stained-glass window of Jesus on the Cross. Suddenly it came to me that, as he hung on the cross, Jesus expressed pessimism.

He said, "It is finished." It is not unlikely that he thought his great work was over and that he had failed. Again he said, "My God, my God, why hast thou forsaken me?" Again there was the deep note of despair. These words spoken in pain and torment did not express the real Jesus. The life he lived was deeply optimistic. He said, "I came that ye might have life and that ye might have it more abundantly." Through the force of his living and teaching, he gave immortal momentum to ideas and ideals that are gaining in power with each passing year.

Jesus lived a life of dynamic, triumphant optimism. He believed, preached, demonstrated and died for the most optimistic principle that man has ever known—that God is love.

The pattern of the life of Jesus was basically optimistic. To discover that even this supreme personality did know despair draws him nearer to us. It gives us courage to go on living with deep optimism through our own dark moments. And it gives us inspiring evidence that deep optimism has eternal influence in the world.

Emerson once wrote this significant statement: "What you are . . . thunders so that I cannot hear what you say to the contrary." The words a man speaks, whether pessimistic or optimistic, or a combination of both, matter little. Not a man's occasional, surface and superficial thoughts, not what he is now and then, but his deep *con-*

tinuing way of living day after day after day is what counts. The way he thinks day by day. The way he acts day by day. The deep pattern, trend, design of his life. The fundamental way in which he responds to life in his minute-by-minute living. The way he bounces back when he falls or fails. These are the tests of a man's deep optimism.

Deep optimism is optimism which has become a deep subconscious habit motivating a man's entire life.

Deep optimism isn't something external that a man can put on and take off like a coat. It is a part of his body, mind and spirit. It is integrated with his whole personality. It is what a man really *is* deep down, inside.

A MILLION MALLET BLOWS

THE late William Ernest Hocking of Harvard said that man is pounded by a million mallet blows from the *outside*. Today those blows are pounding us with tremendous impact. Doubts, fears, worries, uncertainties, problems, smash at our minds and spirits. And yet, here is the great truth that Hocking points out: each individual has the *last word* about how these blows shall modify *him*. "Each one is clay to the potterdom of his group, but not passive clay, not putty; he is *clay with an inner resilience, alive with a bent of its own*. Man differs from other living beings in the vim and deliberate intention of this self-shaping. All organisms do an unconscious job of self-building in the growing process; all animals do a further subconscious work of self-building as they make their way into the habits of their species; *but man alone consciously varies his pattern*. He takes the biological type as an outline; but beyond this he *works as an architect*."

There is inspiration in the fact that those who have taken the hardest blows have been our greatest men. Their handicaps have only spurred them on!

Louis Pasteur was so nearsighted he could not find his

way around his laboratory without his spectacles, yet his discoveries made medical history.

There was Beethoven—stone deaf, yet somehow hearing divine music and writing down his superb Missa Solemnis and the Ninth Symphony. Edison, too, was deaf but turned it to an advantage. He said he could listen for ideas better in the silence.

Steinmetz was stabbed with rheumatic pains constantly and could not sleep without an opiate, yet he became one of the world's great electrical geniuses.

John Bunyan was thrown into prison, and there he wrote his masterpiece, *Pilgrim's Progress*.

Lincoln is the traditional example of a man who started at the very bottom, in a log cabin, and yet achieved greatness.

When William Ernest Henley was only twelve years old he was attacked by a tuberculous disease that tortured him terribly for years. At eighteen one of his feet had to be amputated. Doctors said it would be necessary to amputate the other foot. Henley believed that a treatment developed by Professor Joseph Lister might save his life, and his foot. All alone he made the painful journey to Edinburgh, where his faith in Lister was justified. Lister saved Henley's foot.

In the hospital for twenty months, racked with pain, Henley studied Spanish, German and Italian and made himself a master of French. It was here that the poem "Invictus" was written. Henley felt *within* himself a power to resist all the blows from the *outside*. He wrote the poem as his personal credo:

Out of the night that covers me,
Black as the Pit from pole to pole,
I thank whatever gods may be
For my unconquerable soul.

Women are as heroic as men in battling the mallet blows of life.

Sarah Bernhardt kept on as an actress even after the amputation of one of her legs. She had a motto that she kept constantly in mind—a motto that is worthy of wide adoption. It was this: *"In spite of everything."* She made up her mind not to let anything stop her.

Then there was Florence Nightingale, flat on her back, reorganizing England's hospitals.

And there was Helen Keller, without hearing, sight or speech, graduating with honors at Radcliffe. She even gave thanks for her handicap, writing: "As I walk about in my chamber with unsteady feet my unconquerable spirit sweeps skyward on eagle's wings. I thank God for my handicaps for through them I have found my work, myself, and my God."

Erwin Haskell Schell, late head of business and engineering administration at Massachusetts Institute of Technology, had hidden away in a strongbox a piece of heavy manuscript paper on which were the signatures of a group of graduate students. On the manuscript paper, expressed in three words, is a certain axiom, which, as Schell talked to these students, gave promise of reflecting a precious rule of human conduct. The three words of this axiom create the central theme running through Schell's inspiring little book, *New Strength for New Leadership.* I believe that all those mentioned overcame the pounding of the mallet blows by consciously or unconsciously using the three-word axiom that Schell writes about. The three dynamic words of the axiom are these: *Rise to Difficulty!*

Those who rise to difficulty have a quality in life which might be called "lift." It's the quality airplane builders seek to build into their ships to make them climb faster. It is upward drive. It is going out to meet difficulties instead of running away from them. It is a heroic acceptance of the challenges that come our way. It is the conquering attitude. It is refusing to be buried by troubles, not letting other people get you down, constantly climbing.

Certainly we may have the reaction of wanting to quit, to stop trying, to leave the fight. But we need not be defeated by our instinctive, impulsive reactions. Response comes from deep down inside of us. Response is what we have trained ourselves to be; it is a reflection of our manhood, character, ideals. We cannot always control our surface reactions, but we can sit at the helm of our lives and control our responses to the blows of life.

There are two verses from the New Testament that are especially helpful to recall and repeat daily as we face the mallet blows of life. They are these: "If God be for us who can be against us?" and "I can do all things through Christ which strengtheneth me."

Your spirit is supreme. All the blows with which life may pound you cannot break your spirit. There is only *one* way that your spirit can be broken, and that is if you break it *yourself* by surrendering.

CONSCIOUS EVOLUTION

CONSCIOUS evolution is a conscious personal effort to grow into the man or woman you desire to become.

My grandson has a burning desire to become a champion swimmer. In high school he broke the school swimming record for the butterfly stroke. Still in school, he went on to surpass his own record three times. He finished his high-school career as captain of his swim team, and now in college he is aspiring to make the varsity. His evolution as a swimmer demanded long hours of practice, of exercise, of following rigid training rules. Day after day he concentrated on perfecting his stroke; he worked with devotion and enthusiasm to set new records.

The secret of conscious evolution is to break through the inertia barrier and get started; to overcome difficulties and obstacles and continue to move forward physically, mentally and spiritually. Aldous Huxley put it this way: "Perhaps the most valuable result of education is the ability to make yourself do the thing you have to do, when it has to be done, whether you like it or not."

The man who is consciously evolving is a man who is

directing himself toward a goal. He is not in competition with anyone but himself. He lives by the Hindu teaching that there is nothing noble about being superior to some other man, that true nobility is being superior to one's previous self.

Conscious evolution applies to the whole man: body, mind, heart and spirit.

I've always been impressed with what the New Testament has to say about Jesus, when it leaves him as a boy of twelve years and does not return to him again until he is a full-grown man entering upon his ministry. It gives the key to the conscious evolution of his greatness in a single sentence. It indicates that he evolved in four areas: he *"increased in wisdom and stature and in favor with God and man."*

As Jesus evolved during those eighteen years of preparation for his life's work what was his ideal? What was his goal? Undoubtedly he had the same purpose that he gave his followers: *"Be ye therefore perfect, even as your Father which is in heaven is perfect."*

So here we have the Master's ideal of growth: conscious evolution toward mental, physical, spiritual and social perfection.

Before we shy away from the word *perfection*, let's consider what St. Augustine had to say about it. He wrote: "If thou shouldst say 'It is enough I have reached perfection' all is lost. For it is the function of perfection to make one know one's own imperfections." In striving for perfection we discover our weaknesses as well as our strengths.

Let us now endeavor to apply to our lives the Master's formula for conscious evolution.

Increasing in Wisdom

I like the way Immanuel Kant defined wisdom. "Science," he said "is organized knowledge. Wisdom is organized life." He is a wise man who knows how to live and how to help others to live.

Jesus gave us the key to wisdom when he said: "Seek ye first the Kingdom of God and His righteousness and all these things shall be added unto you." God and righteousness came first in his standard of values. Other values followed naturally. He thought much about the problems of his time and adventured with new ideas about the spirit of man. Through all the years of his development in Nazareth his wisdom of how to express the goodness of God grew and expanded.

Wisdom grows out of our way of living and contributes to our way of life. Wisdom is a product of our relationship with the seen and the unseen.

"The chief difference between a wise man and an ignorant one," said Starr King, "is not that the first is acquainted with regions invisible to the second, away from common sight and interest, but that he understands the common things which the second only sees." Wisdom depends in no small measure upon stretching our conscious awareness of the world around us. It means training the senses to discover and comprehend the wonder and majesty of life.

Our wisdom also grows by associating with the wise. Said Emerson: "There needs but one wise man in a company and all are wise, so rapid is the contagion."

Beyond this the source of wisdom is extrasensory, it is a thing of the spirit. It is having an open self, developing receptivity, insight, perception and inspiration. Wisdom depends not only on outer stimulation but on inner illumination.

A famous philosopher has said: "Man thinks with

his memory." A man is the sum total of the impressions he has stored away. Therefore, in our conscious evolution toward wisdom it is vitally important that we select and control our mental storehouse of thoughts and impressions.

The mind is like a garden. We can consciously select the mental seeds we wish to plant in it. We have the power to grow flowers or weeds. The law of growth will work for good or evil depending on what we plant. Let us resolve to plant thoughts of love, courage, joy, faith, hope, peace, understanding . . . qualities that make for spiritual wisdom.

In addition to sowing wise thoughts we should also sow wise actions. William James indicated the evolutionary process we set into motion by our actions. He wrote: "Sow an action and you reap a habit, sow a habit and you reap a character, sow a character and you reap a destiny."

In our search for wisdom, let us, like Jesus, seek first the highest and the best. Let us strive each day to think, feel and act wisely.

Increasing in Stature

There is no direct description of the physical appearance of Jesus by those who knew him. But I have never been able to accept the frail, pale, weak figure of the traditional paintings. The overwhelming evidence seems to be on the other side. As a boy he roamed the hills of Nazareth and the lessons he learned there were a part of the parables he taught later—the sowers of seed, the lilies of the field, the birds of the air, the foxes, the sheep, the vineyards and fig trees. He spent much of his young manhood as a carpenter, and in those days this required physical vigor. Everything had to be done by hand. The ax was used to fell trees for the timbers of homes, heavier trunk sections had to be hauled out of the forest with ropes, posts were hewn into shape with an adze, strength of arm and back were required to saw the planks.

In his ministry he walked from village to village. He slept outdoors many times, turning his back on the walls of the city. He went often to the desert and mountain to pray.

It took physical strength as well as courage to braid cords of rope into a whip and drive the money-changers from the temple.

It was not only the life he lived but the reaction of people to him that convinces me he was a man of strength. He must have had a compelling physical presence. He spoke, too, with the voice of command. To the paralytic he spoke the ringing words "Take up thy bed and walk!" And the man did. So radiant was his healing power that people thought that if they could just touch his garment they would be made well. He inspired faith. A leper knelt before him and said, "Lord, if you will you can make me clean." When his followers were in a boat with him on the Sea of Galilee, and a storm arose which threatened to sink the ship, Jesus calmed the men and the sea. The men were so astonished that they asked each other: "What sort of man is this that even the winds and waves obey him?"

Most of all I am impressed by the statement Pontius Pilate made when Jesus stood before him: "Behold the man!" To the Romans who admired men of might and muscle this was an inspiring tribute.

Hanging in my study is a painting of Jesus as the whole and vital man I think he was. It is a portrait of Jesus of Nazareth in the full stature of his greatness. It was painted by H. Stanley Todd, in 1932. Todd paints the Master as a dynamic, magnetic personality. There is no weakness here, there is only power and strength.

Here is a man who knew how to make of his life the perfect, unobstructed channel for the power of God; the Master spiritual electrician of the ages.

"He who has seen me has seen the Father," Jesus said. The spirit of God looks out through the eyes of the man in the painting, eyes that flash with power and at the same time radiate love and tenderness. One feels as he looks up at this portrait that here is a man who achieved the high mastery of spiritual law that enabled him to serve as an instrument of God.

Todd's Nazarene is a broad-shouldered man. He is possessed of physical vigor. One can well imagine him at the carpenter's bench or walking with long strides through the countryside. He seems to have tapped the energizing forces of the universe. He knows the secret of recharging his life with the eternal fire of divine inspiration and enthusiasm.

Mind aflame, heart aglow, body atingle, these qualities of masterful manhood are expressed in the Todd painting. Each day I gaze at this painting and find my mind renewed and my spirit lifted. Here is the ultimate in conscious evolution, the achievement of stature in all that the word implies. It sets a goal, an ideal, an image for me to struggle toward in my own spiritual evolution. The finest qualities of manhood and idealism are God-qualities. They were best expressed in the life of the triumphant Nazarene but can be, at least in some measure, expressed in our lives too.

Increasing in Favor with God

One day, during the War between the States, a committee of southerners called on President Lincoln. Their leader asked Lincoln if he considered that God was on the side of the Union.

"Sir," replied Lincoln, "my concern is not whether

God is on our side; my great concern is to be on God's side."

Lincoln was not a churchgoer, but he was a deeply spiritual man. He believed that there are good men in all religions, and as many in one as in another. To live by the faith of Lincoln is to find room for every faith.

Lincoln considered every move and every decision from the standpoint of what God would have him do. He endeavored to be on God's side in leading the nation.

"The only thing necessary for the triumph of evil," wrote Edmund Burke, "is for good men to do nothing." By the same token good will triumph if only good men will take their stand on God's side and work for the good as they understand it. There are shades of good and evil and what may be good to one man may not be good to another. But there is also a great area of agreement on the broad and continuing meaning of love, courage, justice, freedom, peace. When we align our lives with these values we are on God's side.

When we are on God's side we endeavor to convert God's goodness into action, to express it in our lives as parents, citizens, neighbors. It seems to be a spiritual law that the more good that goes out from us, the more good will flow back to us. By expressing the good we set up a magnetic force to attract the good. Thus we grow in favor with the source of all good, which is God.

As we endeavor to evolve consciously in living each day on God's side as best we can know it and discover it for ourselves, we will feel new power flowing into us. As we give of ourselves in service we will find new channels for doing good opening up to us. We will have a consciousness of working in creative partnership with God and may come to know the inspiration and joy which Jesus knew when he declared: "I and the Father are one."

We grow only if we make a conscious effort to grow *outward* into living relations with our fellow men. To grow in favor with men we must reach beyond ourselves. We must develop outreach of mind and spirit. The key to this is to search for ways in which we can serve and cooperate with men in doing the work of the world. We must harmonize our efforts with those of others for the attainment of common goals.

Curious to survey the laws of human relations taught by Jesus, I read through the New Testament several times, marking the words of the Master that seemed to me to have the most significance for our relations with each other.

Reading the New Testament in this light, I discovered that it is an inspiring manual on the art of living together and that it contains much wisdom and insight. I commend its reading to you.

To present the teachings of Jesus in full as they apply to human relations would in itself require a sizable volume. So I have, in this book, endeavored to select the ten statements by Jesus that summarize his methods of increasing in favor with men. I give them to you here with brief comments.

Agree with thine adversary quickly. You must swing into step with a man and move in his direction that you may come to understand him and influence him to go your way, or establish between you a common ground on which you can both stand together. Jesus won men to become his followers when he talked to them in terms of their work: "Follow me and I will make you fishers of men."

And whosoever shall compel thee to go a mile, go with him twain. When a man goes the second mile of his own accord, because he desires to render *extra service,* he has the key to true achievement.

Every tree that bringeth not forth good fruit is hewn down, and cast into the fire. To live useful lives men must be givers, creators. We must bear the fruits of ideas, ideals, services. Our survival demands that we produce, achieve, contribute.

Therefore all things whatsoever ye would that men should do to you, do ye even so to them: for this is the law and the prophets. We are quick to acknowledge that there would be no wars in the world if all nations practiced the Golden Rule, forgetting that many little wars in our own private worlds could be stopped if we personally practiced this philosophy.

Not that which goeth into the mouth defileth a man; but that which cometh out of the mouth, this defileth a man. That which comes out of a man's mouth, his expression of ideas, ideals and attitudes, is an audible key to what goes on in his mind and heart. Spoken words are an expression of the inner man.

And whosoever will be chief among you, let him be your servant. These twelve words express the ideal of leadership in a democracy. Such a philosophy involves not so much a sense of power as a sense of obligation. The great servant is the symbol of the leader.

Feed my sheep. Men have many hungers to be satisfied beyond the hunger for food. Men hunger for appreciation, acceptance, recognition, praise; they hunger to be treated with respect and dignity as individual human beings.

But if ye forgive not men their trespasses neither will your Father forgive your trespasses. Hatred, bitterness, resentment build barriers between men which can only be removed by forgiveness. Forgiveness sweeps the way clear for a fresh start.

Every city or house divided against itself shall not stand. Division thwarts progress. Unity of purpose is the key to progress. Establishing areas of agreement is the first step in settling disputes.

Stretch forth thine hand. To me it seems that the healing command of Jesus to this generation might well be summed up in these words. The open, outstretched hand harbors no knife of treachery. It is the universal symbol of peace, harmony and cooperation.

To evolve consciously in the practice of these laws of human relations is a good beginning in learning to live creatively and harmoniously with our fellow men and to grow in favor with them.

A teacher asked her class to write an essay on what each child considered the greatest thing in life. One little girl wrote: "To grow and grow forever and ever." This is conscious evolution.

We have touched upon the fourfold spheres in which Jesus evolved, with perfection as his goal. This is our task for this life and beyond. Consciously we should keep growing and unfolding through time and eternity.

BECOME A MENTAL
CHEMIST

*L*EGEND tells us that behind Lincoln's life there were three dynamic words of inspiration.

Those three words were spoken to the young Lincoln as his mother was dying. Calling the boy to her, and tenderly stroking his face with her fingers, Lincoln's mother said: *"Be somebody, Abe!"* The inspiration of those words lifted Lincoln from a log cabin to the White House. They inspired him to think, study, grow. Years later the great man said, "All that I am or ever hope to be I owe to my angel mother!"

Three words spoken by a poor pioneer woman worked a miracle.

Each of us has the power to inspire or depress, to lift others or to push them down. We should look well to our words.

Someone has written, "There are no hopeless situations; there are only men who have grown hopeless about them." What is needed in the world is more inspiration. Inspiration has the power to lift men over every obstacle.

There is a passage by Emerson that sets forth a program of action for those who wish to inspire others.

"Don't hang a dismal picture on the wall, and daub with sables and glooms in your conversation," wrote the sage of Concord. "Don't wail and bemoan. Omit the negative propositions. Nerve us up with incessant affirmatives. Don't waste yourself in rejection, nor bark against the bad, but chant the beauty of the good. When that is spoken which has a right to be spoken, the chatter and the criticism will stop. Set down nothing that will not help somebody."

The world needs less heat and more light. It needs less of the heat of anger, revenge, retaliation, and more of the light of ideas, faith, courage, aspiration, joy, love and hope. Arnold Bennett wrote: "The manner in which one single ray of light, one single precious hint, will clarify and energize the whole mental life of him who receives it, is among the most wonderful and heavenly of intellectual phenomena."

I like, also, this word picture of the inspiring personality as set down by Henry Ward Beecher: "Some men move through life as a band of music moves down the thoroughfare flinging out melody and harmony through the air to everyone far and near who listens."

When you inspire someone you become a mental chemist.

If you have a container of water you can change the color of the water by dropping a dye into it. At first there is no noticeable change but as the dye in the water is increased, drop by drop, the color of the water gradually changes.

The thought-life of a person may be changed in the same way. The inspirational chemistry that we may use consists of our acts, our spoken words, our written words.

A friend of mine who is an industrial engineer tells of a change that was made in a foreman through the magic of inspirational chemistry. This foreman was cynical and negative. He looked on the dark and ugly side of everything. His associates decided to try an experiment. Every time the man made a negative statement they countered with positive statements. Every time he became discouraged they painted pictures of courage and hope. Every time he lost faith they renewed his faith. They changed the man's mental chemistry and changed the man. He became an entirely different personality—dynamic, constructive and positive.

A New York publisher wished to put more spirit and drive into his organization. He, too, used inspirational chemistry. He had a card printed for the desk of each employee on which appeared the words: "You Can Do It!" It was the first thing an employee saw as he sat down at his desk in the morning. The cards were also on the walls of the executive offices and in the reception office. The plan was to charge the atmosphere of the office with the dynamic attitude of achievement, to release energy, to inspire greater effort. And it worked.

I know a beautiful young lady with a splendid, idealistic personality. She has given her parents every reason to be proud of her, always. From the time that she was able to read, her parents surrounded her with inspirational elements in the form of books to inspire her to think and grow. They took her to hear inspiring sermons and talks. They endeavored to set an example of plain living and high thinking. On one of the walls of her bedroom they hung an inspiring poem by J. P. McEvoy that this girl read almost daily, and which became a part of her life. The poem is entitled, "If for Girls" and was suggested by Kipling's famous poem, "If." It represented a splendid, inspirational philosophy for girls, ending in these words:

"If you can keep the simple, homely virtue
Of walking right with God—then have no fear
That anything in all the world can hurt you—
And, which is more, you'll be a Woman, dear."

I know a man who read a sentence that changed his whole mental chemistry about being a father. When his son was about six years old this father happened to read these words: "A boy does not have to be shown a mark on the wall to measure up to when there is a man around about the size he wants to be." He decided to so live that his example would be an inspiration to his son. He didn't go off to the golf course and let the son grow up without him. He wasn't "too busy" to be a companion to his son. They played ball together, fished together, read books together, went to the circus together, attended church together. That father raised a fine son through the influence of an inspiring example.

What are some of the inspirational chemical elements that we can use to inspire others?

Appreciation. Pass the praise along. Praise stimulates and results in improved work, for it increases a man's confidence. He feels that he "belongs," that he is on the team. Praise a child's good marks or good behavior and watch that child improve. Praise your wife's pie and you'll have more and better pies in the future.

Vision. Often a man quits because the future is clouded. He feels there is no hope. It is as though he is trying to look into the future through a soot-covered window. Wash the window so that he can see through its gleaming surface into the months and years ahead. Many a young man has been helped and inspired to carry on because someone has shown him the possibilities of the future.

Faith. Most of all we need someone to have faith in us, especially when we meet with failures and reverses. Faith is a steadying quality. When someone believes in us and in the work we are doing we are greatly strengthened. Edison was sent home from school because the teacher said he was hopeless. Years later Edison said, "I won out because my mother never for a single moment lost faith in me."

Courage. Someone has said that beaten paths are for beaten men. Men with new ideas, big plans, great ambitions, noble dreams, need someone to lift them up, cheer them on, stimulate them to dare, to wrestle with so-called impossibilities, and to win. Every new idea, from steamboats to airplanes, has met with ridicule and opposition. But someone believed in those ideas enough to urge the inventors on.

Imagination. Arousing the imagination arouses the creative powers of man. Help a man to see himself as he wishes to be. Help him to visualize himself succeeding. Help him to dream great dreams.

Patience. Men need to be taught the wisdom of working and waiting. Many a man has left the dock just before his ship came in. Time has great power to solve problems. Counsel patience.

Love. The most wonderful inspirational chemistry we can use on another is the gift of our love and acceptance. Devoted and unquestioned love has a magic creative power. The consciousness of being loved is an uplifting, saving, healing force that causes one to go on when otherwise it would be impossible to do so. "Love," said Emerson, "is the affirmative of affirmatives."

We talk about the inspiration of God in our world. That inspiration can come only as individuals like you and me become channels for it. In our behavior, in the words we write and speak, we can become ambassadors of God's inspiration. Whenever we strive to lift up others in ways that are good and noble we are serving as radiating centers for God's inspiration.

All we know of God's inspiration has come through the great lives that have been lived, the great books that have been written, the great music that has been created, the great buildings that have been built, the great pictures that have been painted. The great and good men and women of all the ages *expressed* God. To strive to express the goodness of God is to become a supreme inspirationalist.

THE GOLDEN CORD

THE religion of the future will be a bouquet of the great truths of all of the religions of the world, tied with the golden cord of love.

I have sat at the feet of leaders of the great religions of the world: Christianity, Buddhism, Judaism, Confucianism, Hinduism, Mohammedanism. I am impressed by the fact that most religions are today breaking away from theology, dogma, and ecclesiasticism. They are turning away from the myths *about* the founders of their religions and are getting back to the dynamic truths taught *by* their founders.

There is much that is inspiring in the teachings of the Prince, Gautama Buddha, who renounced his kingdom to go about doing good. "Go into the lands," he told his disciples, "and preach mercy. Tell them that the poor and the rich, and the lowly and the high, are all one, and that all men are united in religion as the sunbeams are united in the sun." And again Buddha said: "If a man foolishly does me wrong I will return him the protection of my ungrudging love. The more evil comes from him, the more good shall go from me." The heart of the teaching of Buddha is the Eightfold Path—Right Belief, Right Resolve, Right Speech, Right Behavior, Right Occupation, Right Effort, Right Contemplation, Right Concentration. Who shall say that following these Pathways will not help a man to attain a higher level of spiritual power?

Judaism was founded by Moses. Not only did his words become religious precepts and moral law for his own people, the Hebrews, but they have influenced all men and women down the centuries.

Judaism has seven basic characteristics. First, there is belief in only *one* God, one holy, all-creative God of love. Second is the concept of historic mission. The Jews believe they are a people chosen by God to render a service to the world by bringing to realization the goodness of God, so that His kingdom may be established. Third, they believe in the ultimate triumph of goodness. Fourth, they believe that man was born in the image of God and they have undying faith in his basic goodness. Fifth, Judaism is a religion of the people, conducted by the people —it is truly democratic. Sixth, it concentrates on making this life a better life. In the seventh place, Judaism is a religion characterized by the quality of growth; it believes in pushing on to new frontiers of the spirit.

Confucius was born around the year 550 B.C. Hundreds of years before the birth of Jesus of Nazareth he gave us the universal Golden Rule, "Do not do to others what you do not want them to do to you." I find much to admire in Confucius because of his attitude toward war. "The greatest general is the greatest criminal," he once said. He was also very practical, remarking on another occasion: "Ideals that cannot be put into human action should not be talked about. To talk about them is merely to wear out your mouth." Confucius taught that evil is lack of harmony, that man should desire to be healthy, wealthy and happy, and to enjoy his days. He taught that the supreme task of the ruler is to make his people happy. He was one of the first men to teach the art of right human relations. He saw that if we have our relationships on a harmonious basis the problems of the world will take care of themselves. He divided relationships into five spheres. First, the relationship between ruler and subject. Second, the relationship between husband and wife. Third, the relationship between elder brother and younger brother. Fourth, the relationship between father and children. Fifth, the relationship between friend and friend. Isn't this a noble objective for all of us?

Hinduism teaches that every man is one with every other man, and all men are at one with the world. It stresses that all things are related through their numberless reincarnations, and that when you hurt any living creature you are hurting yourself. It maintains that the Supreme Being is one, but is called by different names. The Hindu God, Brahma, is the God of all men everywhere. The basic teaching of Hinduism is detachment. The Hindu faces success or failure with spiritual poise; nothing that happens to him touches his deep, inner calm. He is master of the art of meditation. We of the Western world, with all of our surface rushing and frantic activity, might well balance our living by giving more attention to the mystic quality of the East.

The book of the Mohammedans is the Koran. One of the most inspiring passages is by the Mohammedan woman saint, Rabia. It is one of the noblest sentences in all devotional literature: "Oh God, if I worship Thee in fear of Hell, burn me in Hell; if I worship Thee in hope of Paradise, exclude me from Paradise; but if I worship Thee for Thine own sake, withhold not Thine everlast-

55

ing beauty." Living the good life because it is the glorious, triumphant way to live, and not because of the fear of hell, or the hope of heaven, seems to me to be a shining ideal for men and women of every religion.

Charles Francis Potter sums up the Sermon on the Mount preached by Jesus, in six words: *"Act like a child of God."* The supreme teaching of Jesus was the oneness of God and man, the Divine Partnership. "I and the Father are one," he said. He taught that we can only hope to grow when we open the doors of our spirits to the inflow of Divine power—"the Father that dwelleth in me, he doeth the works." And again he said, "The Kingdom of God is within you." And, finally, Jesus gave us his own condensed statement of the substance of both law and gospel: "Thou shalt love the Lord thy God with all thy heart, with all thy soul, and with all thy mind; and thy neighbor as thyself."

There seems to be a growing trend toward the recognition of the good in all religions. Thomas Dreier wrote a stimulating little book entitled, *The Religion of a Vagabond*. In the introduction he says:

One of the delightful things about being a professing vagabond is that you can appreciate the good in all religions. You can associate lovingly with Roman Catholics, Episcopalians, Congregationalists, Unitarians, Universalists, Buddhists, Lutherans, Christian Scientists, Baptists and all the hundreds of religionists with special names. You are unconcerned with labels. You think only in terms of universal goodness. You judge people, if you dare judge them at all, by the quality of their lives. You simply ask, Are they loving? Are they useful? You care nothing about the name they give the religion that sustains them. What interests you is essential spirit—that which is expressed in love.

You associate freely with a Roman Catholic at one time and then with equal joy spend time with a Christian Scientist, or a Baptist, or a Buddhist. You waste no time arguing.

You are never foolish enough to condemn any of them. To you the fact that they exist and persist is proof enough that they are serving those who are members of those organizations.

There is a common integrity of mind that unites all persons of good will. Men who are honest and sincere and loving and intelligent may differ widely in religious, economic, or political concepts and still be good neighbors and close friends. Truly religious people, no matter what religious, political, or social labels they may wear, are those who cooperate with their fellows for the common good of all mankind. To them all persons are members of a common family.

One of the most memorable experiences of my life was listening to Starr Daily tell how the transforming power of love came into his life. From boyhood he had been a confirmed criminal. Although his father remained loyal and repeatedly tried to help him, he continued to commit crime after crime. He said he had no conscience—no sense of right or wrong. He spent a quarter of a century behind prison bars. And then, one day as he was lying in solitary confinement after having been beaten by prison guards, a miracle happened. It seemed that the Nazarene walked through the barred door and stood before him. From the eyes of the Nazarene flowed a tremendous love-force. It changed Starr Daily instantaneously! He began immediately to release love, even to the warden who had been cruel to him. In a few days he was out of the prison a free man, and he remained free. He toured the country many times working with prison officials. He told his story to the inmates of many prisons. He helped thousands of criminals to go straight. Starr Daily told all about this in his book, *Love Can Open Prison Doors*, a classic in spiritual literature.

To Starr Daily the *common denominator of all religions is love*. As we liberate a spirit of creative love we conquer our difficulties, we turn our enemies into friends and accomplish wonders. Daily gave this prescription: "If results don't come at first, *increase* the dose of love."

When we were in Sarajevo, Yugoslavia, my wife and I visited a Moslem mosque. Around the year 1300 the Ottoman Turks conquered this area of Eastern Europe and occupied it for over four hundred years. There are many Moslems here. Beyond the ancient domed mosque a minaret, reaching toward the sky, sends forth daily calls to prayer.

We took off our shoes and entered the holy building. Rich Oriental rugs covered the floor. Beyond the prayer niche rose the pulpit. The leader stood in the center of the mosque and spoke to us in halting English. He repeated the Moslem creed: "There is no God save Allah and Mohammed is his prophet."

So many names for God, I thought as I stood there. Here it is Allah. In India among the Hindus it is Brahma. Among the Jews it is Jehovah. In Japan there are many Shinto Gods. Ancient Greece worshiped Zeus. Egypt worshiped Aton. Jesus called God, Father. Others speak of God as infinite Life, Spirit, Intelligence or Divine Mind.

In the silence of the mosque I asked myself: Is there a universal name for God which will bring men together in a common spiritual purpose? The instantaneous answer illumined my mind—*Love*. The words of the Apostle John echoed in my heart—"God is love."

I stepped forward and threw my arm over the shoulder of the Moslem leader. "Would you agree," I asked, "that all men everywhere should think of God as Love?"

His face lighted up; he smiled and replied, "That is it. That is what the whole world needs." He placed his arms around me and thus we stood together in fellowship, having achieved for the moment perfect spiritual understanding.

Give God the universal name of Love and let it be

symbolized by a golden cord tying together all the truths of all the religions of the world. Would it be too much to dream that religion then could become a force to touch the hearts of all men everywhere?

Many years ago I spent a most rewarding evening listening to the poet Edwin Markham. He was in his eighties then, tall and straight, with white hair and beard. He looked to me like Moses come down from Mount Sinai. He had no tablets of stone, but he recited a four-line poem that was so true, so vital to men, so inspiring, that he, too, must have been speaking for God.

He drew a circle that shut me out—
Heretic, rebel, a thing to flout.
But Love and I had the wit to win:
We drew a circle that took him in.

Perhaps God Himself changed His name to Love in that poem!

SPIRITUAL ADVENTURERS

IN many ways the philosophers are our greatest spiritual adventurers. They are not fenced in by dogma, tradition and theology. Their minds are free to explore the universe and to establish new frontiers of the spirit. Someone has written: "Each man is his own philosopher." To me that means that as an individual I have the right to seek and find the truth that will make me personally free. I am not controlled by the dead hand of the past. I can take truth wherever I find it and weave it into the fabric of my own philosophy. And you can do likewise.

H. A. Overstreet outlines seven major pathways to truth:

First, there is the pathway of everyday experience of life. One meets and mingles with men and learns from them.

Second, there is the pathway of science, using the methods of observation, hypothesis and controlled experiment.

Third, there is the pathway of seership, with its deep sensitized awareness of the many aspects of life.

Fourth, there is the pathway of the prophet, who studies cause and effect in the march of civilization, weighing the future by the past.

Fifth, there is the artistic approach to truth, the seeing eye, the seeker of beauty in the commonplace.

Sixth, there is the method of the mystic, opening his consciousness to the play of the psychic forces, tuning in on the splendor of the Infinite.

Seventh, there is the pathway of the philosopher, which crisscrosses and makes use of the other six pathways to truth. The philosopher uses truth wherever he finds it to build his total concept of the universe and a way of life.

The amazing thing that I have discovered as I have studied philosophy is that there is a great area of agreement between the basic truths of philosophy and the basic truths of religion. In fact, I cannot tell these truths apart. The philosophers have pioneered in discovering spiritual truths that are the essential foundation stones of modern religion.

There are cynical philosophers with a completely materialistic approach to life, like the one who said that our restless search for truth is like groping in a dark room for a black cat that isn't there. And there was Heraclitus, one of the earliest atheists in history, who said: "The world of ours, neither any man or any God shaped it. There is only the flaming thunderbolt that tears asunder and puts together all things." And David Hume said: "I have discovered but one truth . . . that there is no truth." But now and then, even in the philosophies of the materialists, one catches flashes of spiritual insight.

Turn the pages of the philosophers, ancient and modern, and you will find much to inspire you in the building of your own philosophy. Santayana called himself a materialist, yet admitted he did not know what matter is. "Perhaps it is an electric charge," he wrote, "the endless order and vitality of the world in which I live." "God," declared Plato, "created the world because He was good and desired that all things should be like Himself." "Existence," wrote Bergson, "is a process of creative evolution . . . perpetual growth. To change is to mature, to mature is to go on creating oneself endlessly." Herbert Spencer looked upon the world as a machine but confessed it was "a growing machine." The basic idea of Spinoza's philosophy was this: "God and the processes of nature are one." Schopenhauer was a pessimist but found hope for man in this declaration: "The world in which a man lives shapes itself by the way in which he looks at it. What a man *is* contributes more to his happiness than what he has. Insofar as the mind sees things in their eternal aspect, it participates in eternity." Kant, the philosopher of pure reason, at sixty-one wrote his famous essay on religion, in which he defined the real church as a community of people, however scattered and divided, who are united by devotion to the common moral law. "Christ has brought the Kingdom of God nearer to the earth," he wrote, "but he has been misunderstood and in place of God's Kingdom, the kingdom of the priest has been established among us." Xenophanes, the Greek philosopher, taught that God is the mind that governs the world and the body that is the world. He said: "The underlying principle of the universe is God."

The American philosopher Ralph Waldo Emerson has opened doors for me and let in the sunshine of the spirit. His sentences strike the mind like electric shocks awakening men to their divine potentialities. Emerson might well have been speaking of himself when he said, "Not he is great who can alter matter, but he who can alter my state of mind. They are the kings of the world who give the color of their present thought to all nature and all art."

Emerson saw himself as a man fighting with his voice

and his pen to free the enslaved minds of men, to free imprisoned spirits. He gave a daring speech before the senior class of the Harvard Divinity School in which he spoke of a new and mighty faith that should "blend with the light of rising and of setting suns, with the flying cloud, the singing bird, and the breath of flowers." His speech was ahead of his time and it was twenty years before he was again asked to speak at Harvard.

Emerson's fundamental teaching is that everyone is a part of the Divine, and that we only have to plunge within to receive the inspiration of the Source. The Oversoul, he taught, is a reservoir of power, of which every great thought and noble action, the deeds of all the heroes, the dreams of all the poets, are emanations. He wrote: "The life of the soul in conscious union with the Infinite shall be for thee the only real existence. The highest revelation is that God is in every man."

Emerson agreed with many of the ancient philosophers who thought of God as the mind behind the universe, and with the Biblical statement that "in Him we live and move and have our being." "There is one mind common to all individual men," he said. "Every man is an inlet to the same and to all of the same. He that is admitted to the right of reason is made a freeman of the whole estate. What Plato has thought, he may think; what a saint has felt, he may feel; what at any time has befallen any man, he can understand. Who hath access to this universal mind is party to all that is or can be done, for this is the only and sovereign agency."

William James was another philosopher who made a notable contribution to the advancement of spiritual frontiers. James declared that the greatest revolution in his generation was the discovery that human beings, by changing their inner attitudes of mind, can alter the outward conditions of their lives. He taught that happiness depends not so much on what happens *to* us as to what happens *in* us. When we meet life triumphantly, no matter what comes, we have learned the master-secret of living. What we do about what happens to us is the important thing. The worst thing that happens to us may be the best thing that happens to us, if we do not let it get the best of us.

In his book *The Realities of Religion,* James tells about what happens when a man identifies his real being with the higher spiritual something beyond him: "He becomes conscious that this higher part is coterminous and continuous with a *More* of the same quality, which is operative in the universe outside of him, and which he can keep in working touch with, and in a fashion get on board of and save himself when all his lower being has gone to pieces in the wreck."

H. A. Overstreet taught that we live in the kind of a universe that supports the great values. He pointed out that those who accept philosophy as an active experience achieve four rewards. First, they achieve a greater spaciousness of mind and spirit. Second, they have a sounder basis for human companionship. They companion even with those with whom they disagree by entering with them into experiences of doubt, wonder, perplexity and answer-seeking. They learn to wrestle unafraid with the mighty problems of life. Third, they learn to live amid storm and sunshine with poise for they have a broad perspective, the eternal viewpoint. Fourth, they develop standards and values by which to judge life so that they may devote their lives to the highest and best.

As a philosopher looking at religion, Overstreet believed that religion must have two qualities if it is to survive. First, it must be so intimate that it will meet our needs in all the personal areas of daily living. Second, it must be so wide in its outreach that we can never exhaust its possibilities.

Today there is in process a great blending of the truths

of all religions, the truths of philosophy, the truths of science. We are discovering that truth, wherever it is found, is truth, and that it cannot be destroyed. We are lifting our sights to the common goal of spiritual unfoldment. We have become masters of the material; we must now become masters of the spiritual. All the forces that will lift the spirit of man must be put to work. Ahead of us is the golden age of the human spirit. We are entering upon civilization's greatest adventure, the conquest of spiritual frontiers.

CHALLENGE LIST FOR YOUTH

I address this to the young men and women of the world.

You are potentially the greatest generation ever to be born into this world. If you will focus your ideas, ideals, energies and heritage on being creative you can bring about the greatest changes for good in the history of man.

Power is in *ideas,* not in force. Riots are a rampage of ruin. Violence is men out of control; it is a surrender to intense, furious emotion. Wild emotion in the saddle rides roughshod over all the hopes and dreams of men. Force destroys. Ideas build, uplift, expand, renew. The thinking power of our youth can change the world.

The direction in which your lives move will effect the direction of the world for ages to come. Never before has a generation faced so many critical problems. If you fail to solve them the world may not survive. If you solve them you will create a new world.

Mankind looks to you to march forward on a thousand fronts, to lead a great creative offensive which will achieve new concepts, patterns, designs, approaches, in all areas. With so many big, vital, overwhelming tasks confronting you, you have absolutely no time for the small, the trivial, the destructive. Standing on the shoulders of the great men and women of the past, you have the most extended outreach for achievement that man has ever had. You can clutch the problems of your time, wrestle with them and win.

The call is for men and women of heroic stature, youth dedicated to the upward thrust and the onward pace, youth shouting "No!" to the destroyers and "Yes!" to the creators. Daring, confident, determined, you must face the expanding list of challenging things to be done!

The list I am going to give you is filled with impossible things. You may feel that you are too small for them; that they are too big for you.

In *Through the Looking-Glass* by Lewis Carroll, Alice has this to say to the Queen: "There is no use trying. One cannot believe in impossible things."

"I dare say you haven't had much practice," replied the Queen. "At your age I often did it for half an hour a day. Why I often believed in six impossible things before breakfast."

There is magic in believing. The Master put it this way: "I say unto you, if ye have faith as a grain of mustard seed, ye shall say unto this mountain, Remove hence to yonder place; and it shall remove; and nothing shall be impossible unto you."

A peanut is bigger than a mustard seed, but is nevertheless very small.

George Washington Carver, the Negro scientist, believed in the potentialities of the peanut. Through prayer, he asked God to tell him all about the peanut. Then through imagination and research he proceeded to create more than three hundred products from the peanut. These included cheese, coffee, milk, soap, ink, flour, leather stains from intense black to tan and russet, a Worcestershire sauce, a face cream that would take a perfume, a chocolate-dipped confection and a breakfast food for diabetics. By the year 1940 the lowly peanut was the South's second largest crop after cotton, and millions of acres were allotted to peanut production. Carver moved mountains of peanuts and mountains of products made from peanuts because he believed in the impossible.

Go over the list that follows and select six so-called impossible tasks to think about. Or just select one impossible thing and make a decision to devote your entire life to it. Concentrate the full power of your creative imagination on making it come true. If you succeed the world will beat a path to your door, and you will be acclaimed a benefactor of mankind.

Great things are going to be done in the years ahead, and you may be one of those to be listed among the achievers. Consider the fact that at one time the steamboat, automobile, airplane, telephone, television and radio may have been on a list of six impossible things. But there were men who believed they could create these things—*and look what happened!*

We are entering upon an age of great social and spiritual change, and it is going to be up to the youth of today to prepare themselves to solve problems that are larger than man has ever faced before.

To mighty tasks like these let youth put shoulder to the wheel!

Exploring the areas of man's ignorance and teaching him to grow up before he blows up.

Working out new approaches to building an enduring peace.

Launching an all-out attack on all killing and crippling diseases including cancer, heart disease and arthritis.

Clearing the slums and designing and building new cities for modern living.

Harnessing automation for the benefit of all.

Redesigning our streets and highways to make them safe for modern traffic.

Programming the constructive and creative use of leisure.

Making world travel easy, fast and economical.

Harnessing the power of all forms of communication to build bridges of understanding between men.

Making democracy work and demonstrating it to the world.

Researching the psychic powers within man.

Finding ways to distribute goods faster and at less cost.

Developing food for better nutrition and health.

Applying the spiritual dynamic of religion to daily living.

Expanding education to educate the whole man.

Researching ways to control the weather for the benefit of man.

Minimizing the danger of air travel with new devices and techniques.

Promoting a new respect for law as a matter of enlightened self-interest.

Creating a medical plan to keep people healthy, rather than one which treats them only after they become ill.

Looking for answers to the growing trend toward mental disease.

Lengthening the life span.

Solving the problem of overpopulation.

Finding ways to prevent world-wide starvation.

Discovering ways of preventing pollution of air and water.

Exploring the universe through telescopes, radar and space travel.

Establishing world law and world government.

Expanding the peaceful potentials of atomic energy.

Inventing a practical electric automobile.

Designing a new type of plane that can fly and land safely in all weather.

Pioneering new developments in chemistry, electronics and all the other sciences.

Probing the causes of crime and poverty that these evils may be overcome.

Studying man and how he can achieve his personal potential.

Preserving and applying the principles of human freedom.

Harmonizing industrial relations to inspire good will and understanding between labor and management.

Serving the cause of good government by participating in it.

Seeking to contribute beauty and inspiration through the creative arts: painting, sculpture, music, the dance, literature and the theater.

Thirty-six challenges and the list is only started! Perhaps we have failed to touch your own personal dream. Write it down! Write down as many other challenging tasks as you can think of.

What the late Lincoln Steffens said over a quarter of a century ago is eternally true: "Nothing is done finally and right. Nothing is done positively and completely." We live in an unfinished world and there is always much work to be done. But never has there been a time with so much to do!

When there is so much of the high to strive toward there is no time for the low. When there is so much of the big to do there is no time to be little. When there is so much to build there is no time to destroy. When there is so much good demanding to be done there is no time for evil.

Select the areas in which you will serve, then concentrate your heart, your mind, your spirit, on making your contribution to the high destiny of man.

YOU ARE THE HERO

YOU may plan to *write* a book *some day*, but you are *living* a book *every day*.

The Great Biographer is writing the book of your life on the pages of time. Each day is a page. Each year is a chapter.

Visualize yourself striding through the pages of time. Are you hero or villain? Are you big and fine, tolerant, hopeful, courageous, cheerful and helpful? Or are you little, petty, jealous, spiteful? See your life spread out before you in print, in the pages of a book. Would that book be a best seller, attracting people to you, or would it be a book you would wish to suppress? Go off into some quiet spot and think of the pages of your book which you have already lived. Are you proud of those pages? Can you improve the chapters that are to follow? Can you make the ending better than the beginning?

See the words you speak recorded in your book. See the deeds you do between the covers of the volume that is your life. Moment by moment you are building the story of your life. You control your thoughts and acts as an author of a novel controls the thoughts and actions of the characters in his story. No matter what happens to you in the pages of time, you have the power to react like a hero!

Alexandre Dumas wrote: "All the world cries: 'Where is the man who will save us?' Don't look so far for this man; you have him at hand. This man, it is you, it is I, it is each one of us." The reason progress is slow is that we always expect other men to be the heroes and to live the heroic lives. But we all have hero stuff in us. In our sphere of life we can always live more heroically and triumphantly, and grow in heroic stature.

Our task is to discover the heroic qualities in ourselves. James Whitcomb Riley, the poet, once said, "When you awaken some morning and hear that somebody or other has been discovered, you can put it down as a fact that he discovered himself years ago—since that time he has been toiling, working, and striving to make himself worthy of general discovery." Explore your mind, discover yourself, then give the best that is in you to your age and to your world. There are heroic possibilities waiting to be discovered in every man.

To be a hero, it is not necessary to climb Mount Everest, or lead an army to victory. There is opportunity for heroic living in the humblest spots on earth—in your business, in your home, in your church, in your school, and in your village, town or city.

Booker T. Washington, the great Negro educator, told the story of the old sailing ship, blown off its course, lost, and in desperate need of fresh water. One day when hope seemed almost gone, another ship was sighted.

"Water, water, we die of thirst!" they signaled.

"Cast down your buckets where you are," came back the reply.

Thinking their signal misunderstood, they repeated

their appeal. Again came the answer, "Cast down your buckets where you are."

A bucket was lowered. It came up filled with sweet water. For several days they had been drifting off the mouth of the Amazon, whose mighty flood spreads far out of sight of land before it is conquered by the sea.

Cast down your buckets where you are! Start being a hero wherever life finds you today. There is no need of changing your work. There is no need of waiting until some future time. Start living heroically *now*.

Jesus of Nazareth, who made the most heroic impact on the recorded history of man, never traveled a hundred miles from the place of his birth.

The heroes of fiction are not all swashbuckling adventurers. For instance, there is Abbie, the pioneer woman in Bess Streeter Aldrich's story "A Lantern in Her Hand." Abbie is a character who never traveled far and yet developed bigness of heart and soul and mind, and lived much.

When Grace planned a trip abroad, she asked her mother, Abbie, to come along, that she might have the broadening experience of travel. There is much truth in Abbie's reply.

"You know, Grace, it is queer, but I don't feel narrow. I feel broad. How can I explain it to you so you would understand? I've seen everything and I have hardly been away from the yard. I've seen cathedrals in the snow on the Lombardy poplars. I've seen the sun set behind the Alps over there when the clouds have piled up on the edge of the prairie. I've seen the ocean billows in the rise and fall of the prairie grass. I've seen history in the making—three ugly wars flare up and die down. I've sent a lover and two brothers to one, a son and son-in-law to another, and two grandsons to the third. I've seen the feeble beginnings of a raw state, and the civilization that

73

developed there, and I have been part of the beginning and part of the growth. I've married and borne children and looked into the face of death. Is childbirth narrow, Grace? Or marriage? Or death? When you've experienced all those things, Grace, the spirit has traveled though the body has been confined. I think travel is a rare privilege and I'm glad you can have it. But not everyone who travels is broad, and not everyone who stays home is narrow. I think if you can understand humanity—can sympathize with every creature—can put yourself into the personality of everyone—you are not narrow—you are broad."

Abbie is a glowing example of heroic womanhood in simple, humble surroundings. America needs more heroines like her in real life.

When a man thinks of being a hero he often thinks of riding a white charger and saving a maiden in distress. Actually, however, his heroic living should begin in his own home. The pages of his book that tell of his home life should be radiant with heroic living.

"The place to take the test of a man," wrote William Cowper Brann, "is not the forum or field, not the market place or the amen corner, but at his own fireside. There he lays aside his mask and you may judge whether he is imp or angel, king or cur, hero or humbug. I care not what the world says of him, whether it crown him with bays or pelt him with eggs; I care never a copper what his reputation or religion may be; if his babes dread his homecoming and his better half has to swallow her heart every time she asks him for a five dollar bill, he's a fraud of the first water, even though he prays night and morn until he is black in the face, and howls hallelujah until he shakes the eternal hills. But if his children rush to the front gate to meet him, and love's own sunshine illumines the face of his wife when she hears his footsteps, you may take it for granted that he is true gold, for his home's a heaven and the humbug never got that close to the great white throne of God."

Few of us will do the spectacular deeds of heroism that spread themselves across the pages of our newspapers in big black headlines. But we can all be heroic in the little things of everyday life. We can do the helpful things, say the kind words, meet our difficulties with courage and high hearts, stand up for the right when the cost is high, keep our word even though it means sacrifice, be a giver instead of a leaner, and be a builder instead of a destroyer. Often this quiet, humble heroism is the greatest heroism of all. It is the heroism of true greatness.

Years ago Channing Pollock, the playwright, saw a man on the street in a shiny suit of blue serge. In a flash that suit was changed—in Pollock's mind—to shining armor and he conceived the idea for his play, *The House Beautiful,* in which he glorified the heroism of the common man. He saw this man at his work, in his home, meeting his tribulations with the spirit and courage of the knights of old. He saw him building a business, educating his children and fighting for worthy causes—and his wife beside him was as heroic as he.

Heroism in little things leads to heroism in big things. As Edwin Markham wrote: "Our hope is in heroic men/Star-led to build the world again."

You are the hero of your book and it is up to you to think and live like a hero. Day by day your book grows toward the completed volume of your life story. You can't do anything about the part of your book already written; that must stand. But look at those glorious white pages ahead!

CONQUEST OF CRISIS

WE awaken each day to new crises. Crisis surrounds us. Crisis pounds at our minds for solution. We need to develop a philosophy for overcoming crisis. We must recognize that crisis is inevitable, that it is a part of the growing pains of humanity. We must learn to live with it and to meet its challenge creatively.

The hazard of crisis grows imperceptibly, relentlessly until the crises of war, pollution, hunger, poverty, decaying cities, racial conflicts and crime sweep into our lives like an avalanche. We have been blind to the accelerating momentum of crisis.

For the most part the majority of us accept the world as it is and are so preoccupied with our own personal affairs that years pass before a crisis becomes crucial enough to penetrate our consciousness. The sparkling stream becomes a rushing torrent of pollution before we wake up.

Crisis can only be solved by the use of creative power.

Creative Power and Crisis.   There are two creative keys to meeting crisis effectively. When men have used them they have often been able to reduce, and sometimes conquer, crisis—wars have been prevented, diseases reduced, machines invented, resources conserved. . . .

The *first key* was given by architect Allen Dow, who declared that there is one word that goes to the very heart of creativity. That word is *care*. To solve a crisis we must first *care* enough to pay the price the solution demands in money, in effort, in dedication. The mass of expanding crises that face us today can only be solved if we *care* enough to meet the challenge. When we rise above indifference and *care* enough, we will find a way. *Care* will expand our awareness of the problem, deepen our understanding, inspire us to search in all directions for solutions. *Care* is the winning response to crisis.

I like these words by John Ruskin, which indicate the way we should *care* about our earth: "God has lent us the earth for our life. It belongs to us as much as those who come after us, and we have no right, by anything we do, or neglect to do, to involve them in unnecessary penalties, or deprive them of benefits which were in our power to bequeath."

Care is the creative motivating force that applies not only to crises in our cities, our states, our nation and our world, but also to crises in our private lives. A man who *cares* will extend himself, will make a heroic and determined effort to solve his own crises. To *care* is the mark of creative greatness in every area of our lives. The genius is the man who *cares*.

The *second key* is the definition of the first step in creative thinking given by John Dewey: *a felt difficulty*.

Only when a crisis is *deeply felt* will we be stimulated and aroused to *think deeply* about it. Emotion is the spark that sets a penetrating creative approach afire. Ideas come when we *feel* their necessity and turn the world upside down to find them. New ways of doing things are discovered when we desperately *feel* their vital need.

These two creative keys are in many ways synonymous. *Care* applies to our broad general attitude toward a crisis. A *felt difficulty* pinpoints a specific phase of a particular crisis. It breaks a crisis down into manageable parts, manageable difficulties. Both keys attack the greatest enemy to overcoming a crisis: *complacency*. They stir people up, involve them, stimulate creative thought and action.

As I see it, there are four basic phases of crisis, to which we should apply these keys.

First, present crisis. Present crisis is crisis that is upon us now. It is here begging to be solved today. It is crisis piled on top of crisis; the greatest accumulation of crises man has ever faced.

The cost of solving these crises of modern man is astronomical, but the cost of *not* solving them is utter disaster.

The historian Arnold Toynbee advances the theory of "challenge and response." "Civilization only advances," he writes, "when the environment is just right to issue a challenge to the people and when they are ready to respond to it. Civilization collapses when the genius of the minority is gone."

Because critical problems have been so long neglected, we are now compelled to devise crash programs which will accomplish twenty years' work in five. We must launch dynamic offensives for establishing peace, rebuilding our cities, overcoming pollution of air and water, reducing crime, abolishing poverty and hunger. We must organize task forces which will vigorously attack these crises. Things have gone so far now that only heroic measures will achieve solutions.

But it is not too late if we *care* enough, if we *feel* the difficulties deeply enough. We can do the things that must be done; we can find the answers and put them into action.

Second, instantaneous crisis. This is crisis that is a complete surprise. It strikes like a bolt from the blue. Whether personal or in our city, in our state, in our nation, in our world, its impact tests the character of men. It must be faced with a deep sense of *caring,* for a person, a city, a state, a nation or a world. Alternatives must be thoroughly explored with an intuitive *feeling* for the difficulties involved. The attribute most needed in a sudden crisis is a sense of calm judgment. The crisis must be met quietly, with deliberation, without hurry and with prayerful dedication. Often such a crisis requires personal confrontation with antagonists. Tensions are at the breaking point. One of the world masters of the calm spirit was Benjamin Franklin. In his negotiations with the French Government, and with his own countrymen, he often faced crisis. He wrote a prescription for his own guidance which modern statesmen would do well to emulate: *"Sleepless tact, immovable calmness and a patience that no folly, no provocations, no blunders can shake."*

Third, past crises. Through the centuries vast multitudes of leaders in government, education, medicine, industry, science, religion have faced crises; they have succeeded and they have failed. These leaders live in the pages of history and biography. You can consult them today to help you solve your crisis; you can focus their experience on your problem. Often you will be warned away from pitfalls that trapped other men, thus guarding against the repetition of past errors. Or you may discover ideas, ages old, that can be adapted to modern needs. We often blunder into crises and fail because we have not looked backward for clues to help us determine present and future action. A sense of history gives perspective. *Care* enough to use the past for guidance.

Fourth, future crises. Our concentration on the present moment, looking neither backward nor forward, is what permits crisis to sneak up on us and overwhelm us. Because we have failed to see ahead, crisis has now grown into a monster which threatens to destroy us. Vast resources will be required to solve crises which grew while we were looking the other way.

The most creative approach to crisis is to *care* enough about the future, and the generations to come, so that we will look ahead and *feel* and *solve* difficulties before they become crises. This requires the projection of our imaginations into the future; it calls for *creative vision.* "We have only to raise imagination to the state of vision," said William Blake, "and the thing is done."

In this scientific, computer age we have the facilities and the manpower to deal with future crises. Governments, private industry, research laboratories, engineering organizations should establish resources for dealing with crises to come. We should never be caught again in the situation we confront today.

Seeing a potential crisis threatening our future, and stopping it before it explodes in our faces, is the greatest contribution that can be made to human progress.

Where does the average individual fit into all of this? Mastering crisis depends not only upon the giant pushes of leaders but also upon the millions of tiny pushes of the rank and file of men and women. The world's greatest plan for solving the pollution of air and water may never be executed if it is voted down by the people. Ideas for solving racial crises in our cities, or for meeting any other crisis, are in no way limited to those in authority, but may well spring from people unknown and unsung. We can read, study, think and keep ourselves informed. We can communicate ideas and suggestions to our leaders, we can stand up and have our say in public meetings, we can write letters to the press, we can distribute literature and telephone to explain proposed programs. We can become involved. We can become a part of the solution instead of the problem. Out of our own *caring* and *felt difficulties* we can make our contribution to the conquest of crisis.

Crisis is the timeless moment of destiny. It hangs in the balance and may swing either way. The conquest of crisis is the greatest demand made on the creative spirit of man.

DISCOVERERS OF GOD

IT seems to me that the English scientist Sir James Jeans gave us our truest concept of the universe when he defined it as a *Great Thought*.

All the secrets of science thus far discovered, and all those that will be discovered through eternity, existed from the beginning of time. Infinite Mind has all the answers. When the first man walked the earth he was surrounded by the forces and elements which, properly combined, have resulted in the modern miracles of electricity, steam, telegraphy, the telephone, radio, radar, television and nuclear power. All the chemical formulas, all the mathematical procedures, all the principles of engineering existed even before man discovered the wheel or fire. When Galileo invented his magic tube, the first primitive telescope, the principles existed which were to make possible the Hale telescope on Mount Palomar which enables man to look billions of lights years into space. And as the Palomar telescope reveals no end to the universe, so there is no limit to the unfoldment of the *Great Thought* that is the universe.

All knowledge, all facts, laws, principles, have always

existed, awaiting discovery by man. The first message sent by telegraph by Samuel F. B. Morse gave credit to the proper source—the dots and dashes spelled out this message: "What hath God wrought!"

The Infinite Mind provides a vast storehouse of riches. The supply of new ideas, and new combinations of ideas, can never be exhausted. The supply is limitless. As Emerson wrote: "We lie in the lap of an immense intelligence, which makes us organs of its activity and receivers of its truths." Man is the channel through which creative ideas are put into action. Man is the eyes, ears, arms, legs, voice and hands of Infinite Mind. Through man Infinite Mind expresses itself.

All the progress of mankind can be traced back to Infinite Mind. The towering skyscraper, the bridge that spans a river, begin with thought. The idea of the Empire State Building existed when men were living in caves. The architecture of tomorrow exists today in Infinite Mind, awaiting discovery by man.

We often speak of mental or spiritual healing as though it were a technique entirely apart from medicine and surgery. And yet all healing is basically mental. Every new surgical technique begins with an idea. Every new drug and medicine was first a mental concept. All healing comes from God.

Man is putting together a giant jigsaw puzzle. Civilization already represents millions of pieces of creation.

The jigsaw puzzle of Infinite Mind will, of course, never be completed, but its dimensions will constantly expand as amazing new pieces are discovered; it will always be a growing, evolving picture.

The discovery of nuclear power has been the greatest awakener of man. It has shocked him by placing in his hands the power to destroy himself—a power more destructive than earthquakes, tidal waves, cyclones and hurricanes. Suddenly he has come to see that hate and nuclear power represent the formula for mass suicide, and that hate is the spark that will set off the charge. It is revealed to him that he can assure his continued existence only by combining love with nuclear power. Not only will love make nuclear power impotent to destroy, it will also open new horizons of magical power to save and build. *In a world in which nuclear power exists man's only hope of survival is to be a better man.* Up to this point in history man's greatest discoveries have been made in the realm outside of himself. He must now begin to explore more vigorously the "great within" of man —to discover the secrets of mind and spirit.

The discovery of nuclear power may do its greatest good by forcing us to change the direction of our thinking. Years before the discovery of nuclear power, Charles Proteus Steinmetz, the electrical wizard, called attention to the need for this change of direction when he wrote:

Spiritual power is a force which history clearly teaches has been the greatest force in the development of men. Yet we have been merely playing with it and have never really studied it as we have the physical forces. Some day people will learn that material things do not bring happiness, and are of little use in making people creative and powerful. Then the scientists of the world will turn their laboratories over to the study of spiritual forces which have hardly been scratched.

Somewhere amidst the atoms, electrons, neutrons and protons which make up the creative energies in which "we live and move and have our being" will be discovered the secrets of prayer, character, growth, thought, spirit and immortality. With open minds and open hearts we must put the spirit of man under the microscope. We must carry forward a great scientific offensive to delve into the strange psychic forces in man and discover the answers to the mysteries of the ages. Seers, prophets and sages have given us flashes of an inward power in man blinding in its deep spiritual potential. These flashes must be made to burn steadily and brightly to illumine man's spiritual evolution.

Because all knowledge, in all fields, has existed through time and eternity, Infinite Mind is Master Engineer, Master Chemist, Master Astronomer, Master Physician, Master Psychologist, Master Mathematician, Master Artist, Master Writer, and so on. All that man knows, or ever will know, about anything comes from Infinite Mind. Our role is to be fearless discoverers, to knock at the door of Infinite Mind, to seek the pieces of the big picture. For he that seeketh shall find and to him that knocketh it shall be opened.

There is a poem by Sam Foss, about two boys, that has always been an inspiration to me. There are many, like the first boy, who have lost their God because the God they believed in was too small a God. There are others, like the second boy, to whom the idea of God is a growing idea. In many ways, in my own life and thought, I have tried to think as has the second boy—to have an ever-widening concept of God and the universe. In my opinion we can never think of God in big enough terms. He is bigger than our biggest thoughts of Him. Our imaginations cannot stretch wide enough to take in all of God. God to me is all the knowledge, all the love, all the tolerance, all the courage, all the goodness that exists now, or ever will exist. But that doesn't tell it all; God is bigger than that and we shall go on discovering Him forever.

A boy was born mid little things
Between a little world and sky—
And dreamed not of the Cosmic rings
Round which the circling planets fly.
He lived in little works and thoughts,

Where little ventures grow and plod,
And paced and plowed his little plots
And prayed unto his little God.
But as the mighty systems grew,
His faith grew faint with many scars;
His Cosmos widened in his view—
But God was lost among His stars.

Another boy in lowly days
As he, to little things was born,
And gathered lore in woodland ways
And from the glory of the morn.
As wider skies broke on his view
God greatened in his growing mind;
Each year he dreamed his God anew
And left his older God behind.
He saw the boundless scheme dilate
In star and blossom, sky and clod;
And as the universe grew great
He dreamed for it a greater God.

THE PLUS FACTOR IN
CREATIVE THINKING

OLIVER Wendell Holmes gave us a glimpse of the plus factor in creative thinking when he wrote: "There are one-story intellects, two-story intellects, and three-story intellects with skylights. All fact collectors have no aim beyond their facts and are one-story intellects. Two-story men compare, reason, generalize, using the labors of the fact collectors as well as their own. Three-story men idealize, imagine, predict: their best illumination comes from above through the skylight."

Beyond the psychological approach to creative thinking, there is the "skylight" approach. This is what I would call the plus factor in creative thinking.

To begin with let's take a quick look at what the scientists have to say about the steps in creative thinking. There are four basic steps on which they all agree:

First, there is the period of preparation, saturation or stimulation. To create ideas a thinker, like a manufacturer, must gather the raw material with which to build his product. While he was trying to develop a domestic source of rubber, Thomas Edison read everything he could find on various types of plants which he thought

87

might be used in the process. To think, we must have material to think with. We must gather facts, read books, experiment, talk with people, make notes, saturate our minds with data.

Second, there is the period of incubation. We let the mind rest while the idea develops. Having thought about a problem and having saturated our minds with it, we go off and leave it. We relax, fish, play golf, read, sleep, watch television or go to a movie. As Robert R. Updegraff has expressed it: "We let the problem simmer in our mental fireless cooker—our subconscious mind."

Third, there is illumination. This has been called the "Eureka, I've got it!" stage. The answer flashes into our mind. We may be shaving, taking a walk or reading a story when the idea comes. It is not necessary to be sitting at a desk. Often ideas come best while we are loafing creatively with one eye open for ideas.

The fourth step is verification. We evaluate the idea, check to see if it is sound, realistic, practical; we take the "bugs" out of it.

There we have the scientific approach to creative thinking. Many good ideas have come through following this formula which was basically developed by the German scientist Helmholtz and by Graham Wallas of the University of London. Most effective thinkers follow these steps either consciously or unconsciously. Often one step blends into another; sometimes two of them come at once, yet this is the way the mind works in creating ideas.

But this isn't the whole story. Great thinkers use a creative plus factor. The plus factor is not so easily defined as the scientific approach. It involves either the conscious or unconscious use of a spiritual or mystical quality. From the scientific standpoint of creative thinking, man alone is the thinker. From the standpoint of the creative plus factor man becomes a partner with Infinite Mind. He becomes a channel for spiritual inspiration and guidance. His thinking power is greatly expanded and multiplied. He receives ideas "through the skylight."

Leonardo da Vinci, one of the greatest creative thinkers of all time, strongly recommended the habit of meditation in the dark. He wrote: "For I have found in my own experience that it is of no small benefit, when you lie in the bed in the dark, to recall in imagination, one after another, the outline of forms you have been studying." He often awoke to find his problems solved. It is also pointed out by his biographers that Da Vinci would often stand silent and motionless before a painting for hours, without using his brush, as though waiting for spiritual guidance. He was painter, sculptor, architect, musician, mathematician, engineer and philosopher. Certainly much of his power came through the plus factor.

Walt Whitman's friend and biographer Thomas Donaldson said that when Whitman started a poem he had not the remotest idea how he would finish it. Whitman said: "I just let her come until the fountain is dry." This great American poet made himself a channel for spiritual inspiration.

Haydn, creator of more than one hundred symphonies, said: "When my work does not advance I retire into the oratory with my rosary and say an Ave; immediately ideas come to me." God helped him write his music.

The great industrialist Robert G. Le Tourneau, world's leading builder of earth-moving equipment, used the plus factor in developing complicated mechanical equipment. One day Le Tourneau and his assistants were working on a new machine for which there was an immediate need. They were getting nowhere. That night was prayer-meeting night and Le Tourneau never missed prayer meeting. He went to the meeting, put the problem from his mind, and entered into the spirit of worship. Before the evening was over the plan for the new machine was crystal-clear in his mind.

Nikola Tesla, pioneer in wireless telegraphy, television, the induction motor and much other work in the field of electricity, never used models or blueprints in the creation of his inventions. Complete mental pictures of the inventions flashed into his mind.

Now and then a great man acknowledges that some mysterious power outside himself helped him solve a problem. Gauss, the mathematician, speaking of one of his mathematical discoveries, said, "At last I succeeded, not by painful effort, but so to speak, by the grace of God."

In speaking of a solution to a problem Sir Isaac Newton remarked: "It is made plain to me by the fountain I draw it from." Undoubtedly this great man owed his genius to the use of the plus factor.

The pages of biography and history are packed with evidence of the creative plus factor working in the lives of men. Many who have received ideas have received them in wonderment, not knowing whence or how they came. Personally, I believe many more people pray about their work and their careers than will admit it—many men of action are shy about mentioning God and religion. And undoubtedly many men take personal credit for achievements which they should credit to spiritual forces working in their lives. So when we get into the realm of the plus factor in creative thinking there is undoubtedly much evidence that has not been recorded.

Alexis Carrel, author of *Man the Unknown*, put it this way: "Man offers himself to God. He stands before Him like a canvas before the painter or the marble before the sculptor."

Ruskin said in speaking about the powers of great men: "The power is not in them but through them." He, too, recognized that man can magically increase his power of thinking by becoming a channel for spiritual power.

What we have presented here is but evidence and verification of one of the central teachings of Jesus. He said, "The words I speak unto you I speak not of myself: but the Father who dwelleth in me, he doeth the works." And again he said: "He that believeth on me, the works that I do shall he do also; and greater works than these shall he do."

Although men have developed a step-by-step scientific procedure in creative thinking, no specific formula has been arrived at for utilizing the creative plus factor. As a new approach, why should we not use the creative plus factor as a great spiritual catalytic force to lift and blend the four scientific steps previously outlined? By combining the spiritual and the scientific we can add tremendous power to our thinking and speed up the spiritual evolution of man, on which solving the problems of the world depends.

Let us review the scientific formula and see how we can add the creative plus factor to each of the four steps:

1. *Saturation, preparation, stimulation.* In your search for data use the power of prayer. Ask to be directed to the people, the books, the facts that you need.

2. *Incubation.* Once you have accumulated data and consciously worked on the problem, let go and let God. Release your problem to God with a prayer that the answer will come in its own good time and place. Hold the attitude of faith and expectancy, knowing that God has all the answers, that His knowledge is limitless and can never be exhausted.

3. *Illumination.* Keep your mind open. Have a quiet time each day in which you relax with an open mind waiting for the ideas to come. When the inspiration comes write your idea down in a notebook. Thank God for it and ask

him to bless it and help you to put it to work to serve men.

4. *Verification.*   Pray that you may judge ideas from the standpoints of truth and justice. Realize that only ideas in harmony with God's infinite laws of life are from Him. Evaluating ideas with the Golden Rule standard will eliminate those that are unworthy of your highest purpose.

Here is how you can add the plus factor of spiritual power every step of the way in the process of creative thinking.

A FAITH TO LIVE BY

I T has been said that a man's creed is a monument set up to show where he *stopped* thinking. I believe there may also be a monument to indicate when a man *started* thinking in his search for a personal philosophy of life.

"It makes all the difference in the world to your life," says Mary Ellen Chase, "whether you arrive at a philosophy and a religion or not. It makes the difference between living in a world which is merely a constant changing mass of phenomena and living in a significant, ordered universe."

There comes a time when a man should pause and take stock, make a spiritual inventory. He should evaluate where he stands. From the impact of the wide range of things he has read, heard, discussed and thought about during the years of his life, he should summarize and simplify what has meaning and value to him personally.

This is my attempt to do this very thing for my own satisfaction, and I share my results with you. Of course, I often fall short of living up to this affirmation of faith, but when I fail I strive to come back to it, take my stand on it and try once more.

First, I believe in myself. I do not believe that I am a

chemical accident. I believe that I am made in the spiritual image and likeness of God. That is, that behind the hands that write these words there is a mind that thinks them, and that this mind, this spirit, is a part of the Infinite. I believe in the original goodness of man. I believe that I am a son of God with infinite possibilities for enriching and expanding my life.

I believe that my spiritual evolution depends upon the quality of my thought. Thoughts are building blocks, units of substance—a very real substance—out of which I construct my life. These thought-blocks are spiritual and invisible, but they fashion my destiny. A man is a product of his dominant thoughts.

I believe that as a son of God I am born for victory. I am an heir to the riches of the universe. All that men have thought and dreamed and achieved through the ages is available for my inspiration today. I believe that my role is to be a guardian of man's creative contribution to life and to pass it on renewed and enlarged to those who in turn shall follow me.

I believe that to pray without ceasing means to think good thoughts without ceasing. I believe that the art of meditation is letting God speak to me. "We should be silent," said Emerson, "that we may hear the whispers of the gods." Each day I shall endeavor to find time to be still and listen. I believe that by making my life an open door to the Infinite, limitless power will flow into my life, giving me energy, ideas, wisdom and guidance to multiply my capacity to build and serve.

I believe in being eternity-minded. Man does not have to die to become immortal, he is immortal now; this is eternity. I have always liked the way Dean Harcourt, a character in a Lloyd Douglas novel, expressed it: "Eternity deals with the long-haul. They who are eternity-minded are stabilized. They expect their ship to pitch and roll but they know it will not capsize."

I believe my words and acts will have an immortal influence on those whose lives I touch each day. And I believe that the human spirit will go on and grow through all eternity. These words by Victor Hugo have always lifted my heart: "When I go down to the grave, I can say like many others, 'I have finished my day's work.' But I cannot say, 'I have finished my life.' My day's work will begin the next morning. The tomb is not a blind alley; it is a thoroughfare. It closes on the twilight; it opens on the dawn."

Second, I believe in other people. Faith is not only daring to believe, it is also daring to *act*. When I believe in myself as a son of God, I attribute to *all* men the same quality. This goes for men of every class, creed and color. The proof that I believe this way will be measured by the way I *act* toward others.

Most of our difficulty in getting along with each other can be traced to lack of faith. Husbands and wives lose faith in each other and homes break up. Children lose faith in parents, and parents in children, and tragedy results. Labor and management lose faith in each other and we have strikes. Black and white people lose faith in each other and we have riots. Leaders of governments lose faith in each other and we have wars.

Faith is the only bridge human beings have between each other. Only as we strengthen, reenforce and maintain the bridge of faith can we move over the dangerous pitfalls of prejudice, misunderstanding and fear and reach our common objectives.

Faith calls for risk. "It is only by risking our persons that we really live at all," said William James, "and often our faith beforehand in an uncertified result is the only thing that can make the result come true."

Faith means to trust. I like Ernest Hemingway's test: "The only way to learn whether a man is trustworthy is to trust him." The alternative to trust is doubt and suspicion, which may often seem justified. But where do we draw the line? "You may be deceived if you trust too much," said Frank Crane, "but you will live in torment if you do not trust enough."

As for me, I choose to take the leap of faith—to trust too much rather than to trust too little. I will take the chance of being deceived now and then for the more frequent joy of having men respond to my faith in them. Often all a man needs to fulfill himself is someone to believe in him. Having faith in men inspires them to surpass themselves, to discover their divine possibilities as sons of God. With Goethe I believe: "Treat people as if they were what they ought to be and you help them to become what they are capable of being."

Third, I believe in God. My faith in myself and in other people rests on my faith in God. This is the rock upon which I have built my house of faith.

To attempt to define or explain God is to lose Him, for He is beyond the explanations of men. I write only of what my faith in Him means to me personally in the living of my life.

I believe that God is a power underneath my life here on earth. His goodness undergirds me and uplifts me. I believe that one of the most powerful affirmations in the Bible is this: "The eternal God is thy refuge and underneath are the everlasting arms." I believe that I need not reach for a far-off God in the sky, but that I am rooted in Him and grow upward from Him. We are one.

To me God is all the goodness in the universe, available to me here and now, and it is up to me to help convert that goodness into action. "God is love," but He is infinitely more than that. God is love, hope, courage, good will, peace—He is *all* the eternal, everlasting, indestructible values of ongoing creative living.

With God underneath my life I have the faith to build toward the stars.